DAVID

CASCADE COMPANIONS

The Christian theological tradition provides an embarrassment of riches: from Scripture to modern scholarship, we are blessed with a vast and complex theological inheritance. And yet this feast of traditional riches is too frequently inaccessible to the general reader.

The Cascade Companions series addresses the challenge by publishing books that combine academic rigor with broad appeal and readability. They aim to introduce nonspecialist readers to that vital storehouse of authors, documents, themes, histories, arguments, and movements that comprise this heritage with brief yet compelling volumes.

SOME OTHER TITLES IN THIS SERIES:

The Canaanites by Mary Ellen Buck
Deuteronomy by Jack Lundbom
Jeremiah: Prophet Like Moses by Jack Lundbom
Approaching Job by Andrew Zak Lewis
Jesus and the Empire of God: Reading the Gospels in the Roman Empire by Warren Carter
Reading John by Christopher W. Skinner
Reading Acts by Joshua Jipp
Reading Paul by Michael Gorman
Reading 1 Corinthians by J. Brian Tucker
The Letter to the Hebrews in Social-Scientific Perspective by David A. deSilva
Reading Philippians by Nijay K. Gupta
A Companion to Philemon by Lewis Brogdon
Conflict, Community, and Honor: 1 Peter in Social-Scientific Perspective by John H. Elliott
A Companion to the Book of Revelation by David L. Mathewson
Scripture's Knowing: A Companion to Biblical Epistemology by Dru Johnson
Theological Interpretation of Scripture by Stephen E. Fowl
The Second-Century Apologists by Alvyn Pettersen
The Rule of Faith: A Guide by Everett Ferguson
Origen by Ronald E. Heine
Athanasius of Alexandria by Lois Farag
Basil of Caesarea by Andrew Radde-Galwitz
A Guide to St. Symeon the New Theologian by Hannah Hunt
A Way to Scholasticism by Peter S. Dillard

DAVID

A Man after God's own Heart

BENJAMIN J. M. JOHNSON

CASCADE Books · Eugene, Oregon

DAVID
A Man after God's Own Heart

Cascade Companions

Copyright © 2021 Benjamin J. M. Johnson. All rights reserved. Except for brief quotations in critical publications or reviews, no part of this book may be reproduced in any manner without prior written permission from the publisher. Write: Permissions, Wipf and Stock Publishers, 199 W. 8th Ave., Suite 3, Eugene, OR 97401.

Cascade Books
An Imprint of Wipf and Stock Publishers
199 W. 8th Ave., Suite 3
Eugene, OR 97401

www.wipfandstock.com

PAPERBACK ISBN: 978-1-5326-3147-4
HARDCOVER ISBN: 978-1-5326-3149-8
EBOOK ISBN: 978-1-5326-3148-1

Cataloguing-in-Publication data:

Names: Johnson, Benjamin J. M.

Title: David : a man after God's own heart / Benjamin J. M. Johnson.

Description: Eugene, OR: Cascade Books, 2021 | Series: Cascade Companions | Includes bibliographical references and index.

Identifiers: ISBN 978-1-5326-3147-4 (paperback) | ISBN 978-1-5326-3149-8 (hardcover) | ISBN 978-1-5326-3148-1 (ebook)

Subjects: LCSH: David, King of Israel | Bible.—Samuel—Criticism, interpretation, etc. | Bible.—Old Testament—Biography | Characters and characteristics in the Bible | Bible as literature | Narration in the Bible

Classification: BS580.D3 J646 2021 (print) | BS580.D3 (ebook)

TABLE OF CONTENTS

Acknowledgements vii
Abbreviations ix

1. Introduction: The Good, the Bad, and the Ugly 1
2. Making a First Impression 17
3. Royal Relationships 39
4. Run, David! Run! 54
5. Whose Side Are You On? 75
6. Consolidation and Covenant 87
7. Home Alone 104
8. Family Matters 122
9. Making a Lasting Impression 142
10. David: A Man after God's Own Heart 161

Bibliography 171
Author Index 179
Scripture Index 182

ACKNOWLEDGMENTS

DAVID IS THE BENEFICIARY of much support in his life, whether that is Michal and Jonathan in his early years, or Ittai and Barzillai in his later years. Like David, this project is the beneficiary of much support. First of all, let me thank Wipf & Stock Publishers, Cascade Books, and my editor, Robin Parry, for the opportunity to contribute this volume.

The two institutions that employed me during the time that the work on this book took place deserve thanks: Wycliffe Hall, Oxford and LeTourneau University. Thanks to my colleagues of those two institutions who provided a fruitful and stimulating environment for academic work. I also need to thank my students in my Book of Samuel class from Wycliffe Hall and my Life of David class from LeTourneau University. It was the opportunity to try out some of these ideas with students that led me to believe that this would work as a book in a series like Cascade Companions. My work in the Book of Samuel and Life of David has benefitted greatly in recent years by two key projects: the Book of Samuel Section of the Society of Biblical Literature and the two recent books, *Characters and Characterization in the Book of Samuel* and *Characters and Characterization*

Acknowledgments

in the Book of Kings. My thanks to my compatriots on the Samuel SBL Committee: David Firth, Rachelle Gilmour, Michael Avioz, and James Patrick. My thanks also to all those who contributed to the above-mentioned books. I learned a lot from you. Let me especially thank Keith Bodner, who has been an outstanding partner-in-crime and general encourager.

Special thanks must go to all those who read some or all of this work while it was in progress. To my "lay" readers: Mom and Dad, Lisa Skagen, Rich Van Pelt, and Kelly Liebengood. To my "specialist" readers: Keith Bodner and David Firth. Thank you all for your valuable feedback and encouragement.

Finally, of course, I must thank my family, who are both the support and motivation for my work. To Samuel, Evie, and Annie, thank you for showing me the joy in every aspect of life. To Sarah, words cannot do justice to express my gratitude for your partnership. To quote a favorite movie, "I must've done something good!"

ABBREVIATIONS

AB	Anchor Bible
ABD	Freedman, David Noel, ed. *The Anchor Bible Dictionary*. 6 vols. Garden City, NY: Doubleday, 1992.
AOTC	Apollos Old Testament Commentary
BibInt	*Biblical Interpretation*
BibSac	*Bibliotheca Sacra*
BINS	Biblical Interpretation Series
BBR	*Bulletin of Biblical Research*
BCOTWP	Baker Commentary on the Old Testament Wisdom and Psalms
CBC	Cambridge Bible Commentary
EvQ	*Evangelical Quarterly*
ExpT	*Expository Times*
HBM	Hebrew Bible Monographs
JBL	*Journal of Biblical Literature*
JESOT	*Journal for the Evangelical Study of the Old Testament*

Abbreviations

JETS	*Journal of the Evangelical Theological Society*
JSOT	*Journal for the Study of the Old Testament*
JSOTSupp	Journal for the Study of the Old Testament Supplement Series
LHBOTS	Library of Hebrew Bible/Old Testament Studies
NAC	New American Commentary
NIBC	New International Bible Commentary
NICOT	New International Commentary on the Old Testament
NIVAC	NIV Application Commentary
SGBC	The Story of God Bible Commentary
TynBul	*Tyndale Bulletin*
UF	*Ugarit-Forschungen*
VT	*Vetus Testamentum*
VTSupp	Vetus Testamentum Supplement Series
WTJ	*Westminster Theological Journal*
ZABR	*Zeitschrift für altorientalische und biblische Rechtsgeschichte*

1

INTRODUCTION

The Good, the Bad, and the Ugly

> "David was a successful monarch,
> but he was a vile human being."
> —Joel Baden[1]

> "David is good and evil, hot and cold, lovable and worthy of admiration, frightening in his disregard for the welfare of others."
> —K. L. Noll[2]

> "... my servant David, who kept my commandments and who walked after me with all his heart, doing only what was right in my eyes..."
> —God[3]

> "What have I done now?"
> —David[4]

---

1. Baden, *The Historical David*, 259.
2. Noll, *The Faces of David*, 63.
3. 1 Kgs 14:8. Unless otherwise noted all biblical translations will come from the NRSV.
4. 1 Sam 17:29.

DAVID HAS BEEN CALLED "the first human being in world literature."[5] That's quite a big claim. If it is true, then perhaps understanding David will help us understand something significant about what it means to be human. However, in reading David's story, we cannot help but resonate with Nabal, a wealthy landowner, who asks, "Who is David? Who is the son of Jesse?" (1 Sam 25:10). As can be seen by the above quotations, there are many and various answers to this question. David is perhaps the most well-known and prominent character in the Old Testament. Only Moses even comes close. He is also perhaps the most interesting, complicated, and opaque character in ancient literature. He is the slayer of Goliath, the foil of Saul, the friend of Jonathan, the chosen one of God, the poet of Israel, and the paradigm of the good king. However, he is also the ambitious warrior, the deceiver of many, the raper of Bathsheba, the murderer of Uriah, and the Michael Corleone style mafioso who ends his days by giving his son a hit list. He is, in short, a complicated character. Sometimes, however, in our popular conception of David we are too quick to see in two dimensions. He is either the purely pious pastoral poet who is especially attuned to God's heart or the murderous Machiavellian mafioso whose path to the throne is paved with the blood of his enemies. It is easy to get literary whiplash from the portrayal of David in the biblical narrative.

However, it is not good enough simply to leave our understanding of David as a literary mess, a complex set of characteristics that fails to cohere. Because as strange as his portrayal is, as diverse a persona as he appears to be, he is one of the most important characters in all literary history. It is hard to think of any character in history who has had as big an impact on the world as David. One has to turn to Jesus of Nazareth or Julius Caesar to find someone as

5. Halpern, *David's Secret Demons*, 6.

significant as David. He is the founding king of the nation of Israel, he is associated with the bulk of the psalms in the Old Testament, and God's commitment to him (2 Samuel 7) is both a driving force in the rest of the Old Testament and foundational for our understanding of Jesus. In short, David is a *big deal*.

But David might offer us even more than that. As Baruch Halpern writes in his aptly titled *David's Secret Demons*, "David, in a word, is human, fully, four-dimensionally, recognizably human. He grows, he learns, he travails, he triumphs, and he suffers immeasurable tragedy and loss. He is the first human being in world literature."[6] What does it mean to say that David is the first human being in world literature? In a justly famous essay, literary critic Erich Auerbach argued that biblical narrative was essentially different from its classic counterpart, the epic poetic tradition of the Greek world. He noted that in the Greek epic tradition (and we could include other ancient Near Eastern epic works in this list) characters are one-dimensional; they wear their heart on their sleeve so to speak. For example, Odysseus is wily and clever and Achilles is the personification of rage. In contrast, Auerbach said, "[h]ow fraught with background, in comparison, are characters like Saul and David! How entangled and stratified are such human relations as those between David and Absalom, between David and Joab!"[7] Thus, the biblical tradition gives us more fully rounded characters, with depth and complexity. In David we see "a symbol of the complexity and ambiguity of human experience itself."[8]

---

6. Halpern, *David's Secret Demons*, 6.

7. Auerbach, "Odysseus' Scar," 12.

8. Frontain and Wojcik, "Transformations of the Myth of David," 5.

We live in an era that loves complexity and ambiguity. If *Game of Thrones*, the wildly popular HBO series based on the novels of George R.R. Martin, is compelling in part because of its grittiness, its intrigue, and complexity in the portrayal of their characters, then the David story ought to draw our attention because the author of the David story beat Martin there by a few thousand years!

David's story is an exploration in leadership. It is an exploration in human ambition and human relationships. But more than that, it is an exploration of what it means to live in relation to God. Our story claims, as we will see, that David is a man after God's own heart (1 Sam 13:14). What that means, we will have to see as we study his story. However, David's dynamic relationship with God offers a provocative paradigm for what it might mean to be a person of faith. If David is a man after God's own heart in some way, then, as one scholar has put it, "the question about who David *really* is emerges as a corollary to the mystery of who God is."[9] Perhaps, the more we dive into the character of David, we may understand something of the character of God.

KALEIDOSCOPE OF A KING

So what is it about David that makes him so complex? It is the diverse portrayal of him in the biblical narrative. I had a seminary professor who was fond of saying that if you have a settled theological framework, you should probably avoid reading the Bible, because the Bible is always stranger and more unsettling than we want it to be. It rarely conforms perfectly to our categories. He was joking, of course, but you get the point. The same thing is true of David. If you think you have a settled and simple view of who David is,

---

9. Borgman, *David, Saul, & God*, 6.

Introduction

you probably should not read the David story in the Bible, because it is more complex and unsettling than your imagined portrait of David. To steal the title from a masterwork of Western cinema, the biblical narrative portrays David as the good, the bad, and the ugly.

The Good

According to the book of Kings, God's opinion of David is very high. According to God, David is one "who kept my commandments and who walked after me with all his heart, doing only what was right in my eyes" (1 Kgs 14:8). High praise indeed! Things are going to get messy later on, but for now let's focus on the claim that David is good.

Saul, David's less-than-ideal predecessor, is twice told by the prophet Samuel that he is no longer God's chosen anointed one. In both of these pronouncements, we are informed that God is now seeking someone else. Each time, he says something about the character of the one he is seeking. The first time, he says that the person whom he will choose is "a man after his own heart" (1 Sam 13:14).[10] The second time, he says to Saul that this person is "better than you" (1 Sam 15:28). Eventually, when God sends Samuel to the house of Jesse to anoint one of his sons, we learn that this man is, in fact, David. In the process of Samuel anointing David, Samuel gets an object lesson about what matters to God, and we get insight into the way God sees David. When Samuel shows up to anoint one of the sons of Jesse, he sees Jesse's strapping eldest son Eliab and announces, "Surely the Lord's anointed is now before the Lord" (1 Sam 16:6). God rebukes Samuel, saying, "Do

---

10. We will address the complexity of this statement very briefly below and ask what it means to call David "a man after [God's] own heart" for the rest of the book. For now, we will simply read it in the traditional manner.

not look on his appearance or on the height of his stature, because I have rejected him; for the LORD does not see as mortals see; they look on the outward appearance, but the LORD looks on the heart" (1 Sam 16:7).[11] After making all of Jesse's sons parade in front of him, he finally encounters David, the youngest—who wasn't even invited in the first place—and God tells him, "Rise and anoint him; for this is the one"[12] (1 Sam 16:12). What we learn in these texts is that, from God's perspective, there is something good about David. So, from the very beginning, we are expecting an ideal character, one who conforms to God's expectations.

The Bad

However, David's goodness is far from the complete picture. The biblical portrayal of David is crystal clear that he has a dark side. This can be seen in a number of scenes, but we will focus on two: his actions with Nabal and his treatment of Bathsheba and Uriah.

In 1 Samuel 25, David is on the run from Saul, surviving with a band of outcasts in the wilderness. While a fugitive from Saul, David sends men to a local wealthy landowner named Nabal asking for payment for protecting Nabal's men while they were in the wilderness with his flocks (1 Sam 25:2–8). Nabal, in turn, refuses to pay David's men anything, claiming that he doesn't know David. We, the reader, are left in a bit of conundrum because we don't immediately know who is telling the truth. We will

---

11. There is a fair bit of textual complexity in both of these phrases. For those wanting a scholarly discussion of the textual variants here, see Johnson, *Reading David and Goliath*, 30–36.

12. The ancient Greek tradition of this story, known as the Septuagint, has God telling Samuel here "Rise and anoint David; for this one is good" (my translation), adding further emphasis to the goodness of David idea.

Introduction

eventually learn that David did offer some service to Nabal's men, whether or not it was asked for. So, we likely have some sympathy for David when his request is refused. However, David's response is to plan the annihilation of the whole household of Nabal (1 Sam 25:21–22)! Thankfully, Nabal's wife, Abigail, keeps him from doing so. However, what is clear here is that David has a side of him that is prone toward violence. A "dark side," if you will. He may not yet be in full Darth Vader mode, but there is at least a hint of Anakin Skywalker here with all of that dark potential. As Jon Levenson notes in his study of this chapter, here we see "the very first revelation of evil in David's character. He can kill. This time he stops short. But the cloud that chap. 25 raises continues to darken our perception of David's character."[13]

Another clear example of the negative aspect in David's character is, of course, his famous dealings with Bathsheba and Uriah in 2 Samuel 11. David's sins here are so well known that they need not be rehearsed in detail, but let's focus on one aspect of David's evil actions in this chapter. In the closing chapters of 2 Samuel, we learn that "Uriah the Hittite" is not just a random soldier but is one of David's thirty mighty men (2 Sam 23:39). Thus, David likely had a personal relationship with Uriah, Bathsheba's husband, and possibly Bathsheba as well! To my mind, this puts David right up there with the worst betrayers ever. He is right up there with Brutus, betrayer of Julius Caesar, Judas, betrayer of Jesus Christ, and, of course, Edmund Pevensie, betrayer of the Pevensie children in *The Lion, the Witch, and the Wardrobe*. Not only does he sleep with the wife of a friend, but after that he sends the man back to battle, carrying his own death order. It is hard to picture a colder betrayal.

---

13. Levenson, "1 Samuel 25," 23.

The Ugly

In addition to texts that clearly portray David as good (e.g., 1 Sam 13:14; 16:7) and texts that clearly portray David as bad (e.g., 1 Sam 25; 2 Sam 11), there are texts that are just plain ugly. One example of this kind of portrayal is David's treatment of his first wife, Michal. When we are introduced to Michal, we learn that "Michal loved David" (1 Sam 18:20). We don't know, however, whether David loved Michal. We are simply not told. Scholars have often pointed out that this feels like David is more interested in the status marriage to the king's daughter brings rather than he is in Michal herself. Whether or not this is the case, it is at least possible.

After David and Michal are married, David is forced to flee from Saul and leave his new bride behind. We later learn that Saul gives Michal to another man, Paltiel son of Laish (1 Sam 25:44; 2 Sam 3:15). When David then takes the throne and is in conflict with Ishbosheth, Saul's son, he makes a deal to get Michal back. As Michal is escorted back to David, her new husband, Paltiel, follows after her, "weeping as he walked behind her" (2 Sam 3:16). The picture is heartbreaking. We assume that Michal was at least in a loving relationship and it is questionable whether she wanted to be brought back to David. Finally, in the last scene where David and Michal interact, we see David dancing before the ark of the covenant in a linen ephod, which Michal deems inappropriate (2 Samuel 6). David's response to Michal's disapproval is to proclaim that he will continue to abase himself before the Lord (2 Sam 6:21–22). The narrator then adds the comment "And Michal the daughter of Saul had no child to the day of her death" (2 Sam 6:23). We do not know why that is, but we are at least free to speculate that David had no sexual relations with Michal because they were not on good terms. It is a sad end to a story that started with a young princess who was in love with the up-and-coming David. It is possible to justify some of David's actions towards Michal. She was his wife. Perhaps he has a right to demand her back. She did mock his celebration before the ark. Perhaps he is justified in resenting her. However, it is hard to avoid the feeling that there is a lot of ugliness here.

The biblical text, then, portrays David as the good, the bad, and the ugly. The result of which is that David becomes something like a kaleidoscope and what we see in him depends on how we twist the lens. We may twist the lens so as to focus on the good David, the one who is a man after God's own heart and is the paradigm of a righteous king. Or, we may focus on the bad David, who has a violent streak and is not afraid to take what is not his and murder others to cover up for his crimes. Or, we may focus on the ugly David, the David who is not quite evil but whose actions are at least ambiguous.

CONCLUSION: THE HEART OF THE MATTER?

One of the key issues that we face when we look at the character of David is the discrepancy between what we read about him in his story and some of the statements that are made about him. We are introduced to the expectation of David in 1 Sam 13:14, in which Samuel rejects Saul for not doing what the LORD commanded. He tells Saul that "the LORD has sought out for himself a man after his own heart." We assume this means that God is seeking a man whose heart he approves.[14] Thus, our expectations for Da-

14. This is disputed by scholars, many of whom argue that the phrase "a man after his own heart" means that God is choosing someone *according to God's own choice*, not that it suggests anything positive about that person's heart. For my argument that it does indeed say something about David's heart, see Johnson, "The Heart of Yhwh's

vid are that he will be a man whose heart exemplifies God in some way. The problem is, as David's story progresses, we encounter the good, the bad, and the ugly of David. We are then left wondering what it could possibly mean to call David a man after God's own heart. This will be a question that will come up again and again in our analysis of David.

What we have then in the character of David is the complex portrait of a real human being. As we engage with his story, we'll see that David is indeed the hero and we are meant to cheer for him. However, he often acts in a way that makes it difficult to see him as a hero. And while God's commitment to him is absolute, the narrative's approval of him is not. This raises the very difficult question of just what it means to call David a man after God's own heart. If there is something in David's heart that makes him uniquely qualified to function as God's chosen one, then he is a character to be emulated. The David we see revealed in the story, however, is one that is difficult to want to emulate. We are left puzzling just what it is about David that may make him a man after God's own heart. It is this question that we will try to address throughout this book.

EXCURSUS: STRANGER THAN FICTION, TRUER THAN HISTORY

Though this book is on David as he is portrayed in biblical literature, it will also help us to discuss the biblical portrait of David by asking historical questions of it. There is virtually no aspect of the biblical portrayal of David that is not questioned by scholars. Views of the biblical portrait of David range from the view that it is probably largely

---

Chosen One." For differing views, see Athas, "A Man after God's Own Heart"; and DeRouchie, "The Heart of Yhwh and His Chosen One."

Introduction

historically reliable[15] to the view that it has little if any relationship to history.[16] That's quite a range of possible views!

Before looking at the evidence for David, we need to ask two questions of methodology. The first is the question of posture. When we come to the biblical text, we can either *assume* it is basically historically accurate unless strong evidence suggests otherwise (this is known as the *principle of falsification*), or, we can *doubt* that the biblical text is historically accurate unless it is proven to be so by other sources (this is known as the *principle of verification*). As you can imagine, which approach you take greatly affects the way you view the historical reliability of the Bible.

The next question is: What kind of literature do we have in the story of David? Obviously, if it does not intend to be a historical narrative, it would be inappropriate to treat it as such. Not all of the Bible is equally intended to be a historical narrative. The Book of Kings, for example, is very clearly trying to give an historical account. On the other hand, it is not clear that the Book of Job even intends to be an historical account. When it comes to the Book of Samuel, there is no question, to my mind at least, that the David story has been treated as historical for as long as it has been read. However, the mode in which it operates is certainly primarily a literary mode. Does that mean it is not historical? No. It turns out that our mode for doing history is in narrative form. It is thus helpful to think of the portion of Scripture from Joshua through Kings as some form of literary representation, or a portrait, of the past.[17] The portrait

---

15. E.g., Provan, Long, and Longman, *A Biblical History of Israel*.

16. E.g., Davies, *In Search of 'Ancient Israel.'*

17. For good discussions of history and narrative representation see Barstad, *History and the Hebrew Bible*, 1–38; Gilmour, *Representing the Past*, 1–39; and Provan, Long, and, Longman, *A Biblical History of Israel*, 59–134.

is not the thing itself, but it is an interpreted representation of the thing itself. It is my suggestion that what we have in the David story is a literary representation that offers an interpretation of the significance of the David of history.

Non-Biblical Testimony Related to David

The starting point for non-biblical testimony to the historical David is the Tel Dan Inscription. It is an Aramean inscription telling of military victories of an Aramean king from the ninth century that refers to Judah as "the house of David."[18] The significance of this text is that it shows that a century and a half after David would have lived, a foreign king knew David as the historical character that founded the dynasty of Judah. While this does not prove the historicity of the David story in the Bible, it is a crucial foundation stone.

A second place to look for non-biblical testimony to the historical David is evidence from tenth-century Jerusalem, which, according to the biblical testimony, became David's capital. There is much debate surrounding the archaeological record of Jerusalem. Two key pieces of potential evidence are the monumental architecture known as the "Stepped Stone Structure" and the "Large Stone Structure." The first is a series of stone terraces and a large mantle wall on the eastern side of the hill of the Old City of David in Jerusalem, which has been associated by some as the "Millo" that is part of David's city (see 2 Sam 5:9). The latter is a large building on the summit of the hill to the west of the "Stepped Stone Structure." If these two structures date to the tenth century, and they are related, then we have

---

18. For a good recent discussion with the text see, Knapp, *Royal Apologetic*, ch. 7.

something of a "citadel complex" in the Old City of David.[19] This complex shows that tenth-century Jerusalem would have been "a rather small town with a mighty citadel, which could have been a center of a substantial regional polity."[20] This, then paints a portrait of Jerusalem, that would fit what we see in the David story.

Finally, there is Khirbet Qeiyafa, a fortified town along the Elah Valley in the Western Shephelah. It is significant because if it is a Judahite town, possibly the biblical city of Sha'arim (see 1 Sam 17:52), then it supports the biblical narrative, which paints a picture of a significant political entity in Israel that had a significant military outpost right on the border with the Philistine territory. Furthermore, an ostracon (a broken piece of pottery with writing on it) found at Khirbet Qeiyafa looks like it may have Hebrew writing (or at least early Semitic writing) and is likely a school text. While some scholars have doubted the possibility of written records that could go back to the time of David, this ostracon shows evidence of a writing culture in early Israel.[21]

Committing an Act of Historical Imagination

Have we proven the historical accuracy of the David story? No. What have we done then? We have shown that within a century and a half of his life, it was widely known that a

---

19. See the claims of the excavator, E. Mazar, *The Palace of King David*. For a brief critique, see Becking, "David between Evidence and Ideology," 11–12.

20. A. Mazar, "Archaeology and the Biblical Narrative," 46.

21. There is a lot of literature on this. On Khirbet Qeiyafa generally, see Becking, "David between Evidence and Ideology," 11–12; and Dever, *Beyond the Texts*, 285–88. On the ostracon, specifically, see Millard, "The Ostracon from the Days of David"; Galil, "The Hebrew Inscription"; and Becking and Sanders, "Plead for the Poor and the Widow."

character named David was the founder of the dynasty of Judah. Also, though this is by no means indisputable, we have shown that the archaeological finds in Jerusalem and Khirbet Qeiyafa show a tenth-century culture that fits with the David story, which allows the biblical narrative to be at least plausible. What then do we do with this information?

Any attempt to understand what happened in the past requires an act of historical imagination. The truth is, we have no direct access to the past. We have only testimonies. What we have then are testimonies to the story of David both written and archaeological and we have to commit an act of historical imagination based on those testimonies. On the basis of the range of historical information available what we find is this. A majority of scholars, from a wide range of backgrounds, think it is very likely that the historical David was some sort of chieftain or warlord and probably had a base of operations at Hebron and then expanded it to Jerusalem. He established a dynasty that likely exercised a degree of influence in the surrounding area that would eventually become the kingdom of Judah.[22]

In his recent massive work on the Bible and archaeology, William Dever, a preeminent archaeologist, offers his assessment of the relationship between the biblical account of David and the archaeological record as follows:[23]

---

22. For a fuller presentation of this see, Johnson, "Israel at the Time of the United Monarchy," esp. 509–10.

23. From Dever, *Beyond the Texts*, 342, Fig. 4.28.

Biblical narratives analyzed in the light of the archaeological data for the late eleventh–tenth century		
Proven	Unproven but possible	Disproven
- collaboration with the Philistines - charismatic leader - dynastic murders - dynasty founder - building up Jerusalem - Philistines as threat	- "David's Citadel" - defeat of Philistines - war with Arameans - defeat of Ammonites, Moabites, and Edomites	- border to Euphrates

The interesting fact about the above reconstruction of the David story and the archaeological assessment of Dever is that they essentially cohere with the major narrative framework of the biblical story of David. From where I sit, I see no reason to question the broad narrative framework of the David story, even if we are willing to sit lightly to some of the details as interpretive. After all, treating this text as Sacred Scripture means that the interpretive details are just as important or perhaps more important than the bare historical facts, if we can use such a term. It is in the interpretive details that the writer of the David story leads us into the truth of David, which transcends the mere historicity of David. The story addresses much bigger issues of who God is and how he interacts with his people. Therefore, the significance of David goes far beyond a mere list of historical deeds. Perhaps, in the end, the truth about David is stranger than fiction and truer than history.

QUESTIONS FOR REFLECTION

1. What is your general picture of David? Do you think of him in mostly positive or negative terms? What do you associate most with him?
2. Think of other scenes or aspects of the David story that you know. Do they portray David as good, bad, or ugly?
3. What do you think it means to be "a man after God's own heart"? How does what you think it means relate to the characterization of David?
4. Does the limited historical testimony to David change your view of the biblical narrative? Why or why not?

2

MAKING A FIRST IMPRESSION

1 Samuel 16–17

> "Rise and anoint him; for this is the one."
> —God[1]

> "whose son is this young man?"
> —Saul[2]

As the saying goes, you never get a second chance to make a first impression. Unless, of course, like David, you get a first introduction, then a second one, then a third one, etc. Readers of David's story have long noticed that there seem to be multiple introductions to David as he comes on the scene in 1 Samuel 16–17. In this chapter we will look at

1. 1 Sam 16:7.
2. 1 Sam 17:55.

these various introductions to him and see what they say about him as a character. Included in these stories is one of the most famous stories in the Bible, the iconic confrontation between David and Goliath. In these introductory chapters David's stock is clearly on the rise. However, we will see that even in these early chapters David is a bit more complex than he may appear at first glance.

SEEING DAVID (1 SAMUEL 16)

God and Samuel See David (1 Samuel 16:1–13)

> The LORD said to Samuel, "How long will you grieve over Saul? I have rejected him from being king over Israel. Fill your horn with oil and set out; I will send you to Jesse the Bethlehemite, for I have provided for myself a king among his sons."
>
> (1 Sam 16:1)

The story up to this point has been the rise and fall of king Saul, from his selection as king by the prophet Samuel (1 Samuel 9) to his brief military success (1 Samuel 11) to his ultimate rejection (1 Samuel 13 and 15). The previous episode in the narrative was Samuel's unequivocal rejection of Saul. Now in chapter 16 it is clear that the narrator wants us to read the introduction to David as a response to the rejection of Saul. The first verse of chapter 16 picks up the theme of rejection as God tells Samuel "I have rejected him [Saul] from being king over Israel" (1 Sam 16:1; cf. 15:23).

In addition to preparing to introduce us to David against the backdrop of the rejection of Saul, the first verse of chapter 16 sets up the key theme that will play throughout the chapter. The NRSV translates God's words as "I have *provided* for myself a king among his [Jesse's] sons." The word the NRSV translates as "provided" is the Hebrew word *r'h*, which literally means "see." So a more literal translation would be, "I have *seen* for myself a king among his sons." It is important to note this because the word "see" (Heb. *r'h*) will be used throughout chapter 16 and create something of a theme. There will be a lot of *seeing* in this chapter and we will have to ask whether we are all *seeing* the same thing.

God tells Samuel to go to the house of Jesse to see and anoint the new king. But Samuel objects because he is afraid that if Saul hears about this, he will kill him (16:2). Samuel's concern is probably a fair one. It is probably fair to say that the fact that a king would not respond well to someone anointing their replacement could be considered a truth universally acknowledged. So, God provides a little cover for Samuel. He tells him to bring a heifer with him and tell people that he is going to Bethlehem to sacrifice to the LORD and maybe he just happens to invite Jesse and his family as well (16:2–3). The literary play in this ruse is interesting. Both instances where Saul was rejected by God involved sacrifice. In the first instance, Saul was accused of some sort of inappropriate sacrifice (1 Samuel 13). In the second instance, Saul claimed that the reason that he did not obey God's command and put all the animals to death was that they were being kept to sacrifice to the LORD (1 Sam 15:15, 21). He is reprimanded for this by Samuel. Now, after two instances of inappropriate sacrifice, Saul's replacement is going to be anointed under the guise of a sacrifice. One cannot help but see the poetic irony of this. We may perhaps be permitted to think of God subtly communicating that, "two can play at this 'it's for a sacrifice' game!"

When Samuel arrives at the house of Jesse, he immediately *sees* Eliab and thinks that surely this strapping young lad is the LORD's anointed. God's response to him is significant.

> "Do not *look* on his *appearance* or on the height of his stature, because I have rejected him; for the LORD does not *see* as mortals *see*; they *look* on the outward *appearance*, but the LORD *looks* on the heart."
>
> (1 Sam 16:7)

Here the focus of the *seeing* theme in this chapter comes to the foreground and the key insight is the difference between divine seeing and human seeing. God can see what no person can see. God can see into the inner person, that which is hidden from human sight. The implication, once David is chosen, is that there is something in David, unseen by human eyes, that God judges to be appropriate for leadership. He must have some interior quality that makes him right to be God's chosen king.

Of course, after God has made it very clear that he judges based on the heart and not on external features, the natural thing would be to get a detailed physical description of God's chosen one, right? This would be a bit like Simon Cowell announcing that he wasn't judgmental before obliterating one of his contestants. The one thing seems to invalidate the other. So, what are we to do with the fact that God announces that he sees the heart not the outward appearance before learning detailed physical information about David?

In the Old Testament characters are rarely described in physical detail. When they are, it is always significant for the narrative. It is significant that Joseph is described as handsome (Gen 39:6), because that gets him into trouble in Potiphar's house (Gen 39:7–20). It is significant that Rachel is described as beautiful (Gen 29:17), because that is related to the rivalry between her and Leah (Gen 29:31—30:24). It is, of course, significant that Goliath is given significant physical description (1 Sam 17:4-8) as we will see below.

Making a First Impression

So, the fact that the narrator reports a detailed description of David's physical features must be significant. This is especially true given the theme of seeing in the chapter. We have been told that God *has seen* a son of Jesse who will be king. We are then told that Samuel *saw* Eliab's appearance and assumed he was the one. God then corrects Samuel by stating that what matters is not the outer appearance, which humans *see*, but the heart, which God *sees*. Then the reader is given an opportunity to *see* David in all his external glory!

Scholars have puzzled with what to make of the fact that we are given such detail about David's physical description. Most scholarly strategies for interpreting David's attractiveness assume that the descriptions of David are overwhelmingly positive. However, that is not entirely certain.

> Now he was ruddy, and had beautiful eyes, and was handsome.
> (1 Sam 16:12)

Although the three descriptors used for David seem positive, it is not clear that they are the expected features one would want in a good candidate for king. First of all, it is interesting to contrast the physical description of Saul, who seems at least to look the part of king,[3] with David. Saul (and Eliab, for that matter) is described in terms of his height and size (1 Sam 9:2; 10:23). David, on the other hand, is not described by his size, but his appearance. First, David is ruddy. Other than David, the only other biblical characters that are described this way are the *infant* Esau (Gen 25:25) and the beloved in the Song of Songs (Song 5:10). Second, David has beautiful eyes. Though this exact

---

3. This seems evident by Samuel's apparent brag about Saul. "Samuel said to all the people, 'Do you see the one whom the LORD has chosen? There is no one like him among all the people.' And all the people shouted, 'Long live the king!'" (1 Sam 10:24).

phrase is used nowhere else, the description of "beautiful" is regularly used of women in the Old Testament.[4] The only men who are described with this word are Joseph (Gen 39:6) and Absalom (2 Sam 14:25). For both of them their beauty becomes a problem. Third, David is handsome. Again, this kind of description is used regularly of women in the Old Testament.[5] Thus, while David's physical appearance seems to characterize him positively, it is a slightly complicated characterization. Thus, as one scholar has argued, perhaps in his physical description we ought to see that "[r]ather than 'ruddy and virile,' [David] was pink and pretty."[6] He may be more boyish than manly, more model than monarch. Even though David's physical appearance is positive, it makes him a somewhat surprising candidate for warrior king. This would make sense if one of the points of this chapter is to say that God doesn't choose based on external features but internal ones.

Once David is on the scene and duly described to us, Samuel anoints him (16:13a). The consequence of his anointing is that "the spirit of the LORD came mightily upon David from that day forward" (16:13b). Though the spirit of the LORD has energized other leaders (Samson: Judg 14:6, 19; 15:14; Saul: 1 Sam 10:10; 11:6), the spirit of the LORD comes on David *from that day forward*. David is thus contrasted with previous leaders like Samson and Saul who had the spirit come upon them several times, as if it was an intermittent experience. David, on the other hand, seems to be described as receiving the spirit of the LORD in a more

---

4. For example, it is used to describe Sarah (Gen 12:11, 14); Rachel (Gen 29:17); Abigail (1 Sam 25:3); Tamar (2 Sam 13:1); Abishag (1 Kgs 1:3); and Esther (Esth 2:7).

5. For example, it is used to describe Rebekah (Gen 24:16; 26:7), Bathsheba (2 Sam 11:2), Queen Vashti (Esth 1:11), Esther (Esth 2:7).

6. Greenspahn, *When Brothers Dwell Together*, 88.

permanent way. The theme of God's presence with David will become a theme throughout his story, but especially in these early chapters (16:18; 18;12, 14, 28). We have thus had our first introduction to David. It has been a complicated one, but it has affirmed the quality of his heart and the presence of God with him.

Saul and His Servants See David (1 Samuel 16:14–23)

With the spirit of God now with David, it appears that it can no longer be with Saul and now "an evil spirit from the LORD tormented him" (16:14).Though the concept of "an evil spirit from the LORD" is a difficult one, the key point here appears to be that the spirit of the LORD is now disastrous toward Saul rather than beneficial.[7] The significant part of this setting for our understanding of David is that the anointing of David and the imparting of the spirit upon him has caused a new spiritual problem for Saul, one that needs solving.

The surprise here is that Saul's servants are spiritually perceptive enough to recognize Saul's spiritual problem. They manage to diagnose it and to proscribe a cure (16:15–16). The significance of the spiritual perceptiveness of Saul's servants is that we, the readers, are clued in to pay attention to their words because we know that they have insight into the situation.[8] Their proposal is to seek a musician who can play music and soothe Saul (16:16). Saul agrees and tells them to "*See*[9] for me someone who can play well" (16:17).

---

7. For attempts to wrestle with this issue see Tsumura, *First Book of Samuel*, 427–28, and Routledge, "An Evil Spirit from the Lord."

8. On this point, and the rest of this scene see Johnson, "David Then and Now."

9. The NRSV translates this: "provide." However, it is the key word "see" (*r'h*) that we have been tracing.

One of Saul's servants speaks up and utters the statement that is most important for our understanding of David.

> "I have seen a son of Jesse the Bethlehemite who is skillful in playing, a man of valor, a warrior, prudent in speech, and a man of good presence; and the LORD is with him."
>
> (1 Sam 16:18)

We have been doing a lot of *seeing* in this chapter and a lot of it has been focused on David. Now, through the eyes of this nameless servant, we are invited to *see* David again. However, what we *see* is not what one would expect to *see* in a young shepherd boy. For that reason, this verse has given interpreters trouble. It is clearly a resumé for David. However, how appropriate is it to call a young shepherd boy who will soon complain that he doesn't know how to use conventional armor (17:39) a "man of valor" or a "warrior"? There are a number of ways that we could understand this. I think the most helpful is to see these descriptions as somewhat double-voiced. In other words, each description of David could make sense in the narrative context in which it stands, but it also foreshadows what David will ultimately become. David is currently "skillful in playing." This is true of David in this context. However, David will continue to gain fame as a songwriter in the Book of Samuel (e.g., 2 Samuel 1, 22) and his connection to the book of Psalms shows just how pervasive this connection is. David can currently be described as a "man of valor" if that is understood in the sense of someone who is of a certain kind of social standing. It is perhaps a commentary on the prominence of his family. On the other hand, David and his military prowess will certainly earn him the label "man of valor" in the fullest sense of the word. Despite numerous popular depictions of David as a little boy, he can currently be described

Making a First Impression

as a "warrior" if that is understood in the sense of someone who is of age to serve militarily. On the other hand, like the phrase "man of valor," David will eventually own the title of "warrior" in every sense of the word, and it is not always a positive characterization. The descriptions of David as "prudent in speech" and a "man of good presence" can also be understood as describing the young David, but also foreshadow his future characterization. He will soon prove himself to be a man fully capable of clever speech (e.g., 17:45–47, 24:14) and we already know that he is a man of good form, which perhaps foreshadows how characters will be drawn to him throughout the narrative.

We are thus introduced to David this second time and given his professional resumé. This resumé can be understood in its current context, but it also points forward to aspects of his character that we will find to be true in different ways throughout his story. In short, we are introduced to David here in the second half of chapter 16 in such a way that has significant forward-pointing energy.

> And David came to Saul, and entered his service. Saul loved him greatly, and he became his armor-bearer.
> (1 Sam 16:21)

Although the NRSV says "Saul loved him greatly" the Hebrew text simply reads "He love him greatly" and leaves it up to the reader to supply the subject of the pronoun. It could be that David loved Saul or it could be that Saul loved David. Though the fact that Saul loved David would make more sense in the narrative context where everyone will love David, both are possible. The important thing to note is that however contentious and antagonistic this relationship becomes, it starts as a relationship that is characterized in some way by love.

With David now firmly established in Saul's court, the narrative sums up David's role as the one who would play the lyre and bring Saul relief whenever an evil spirit would come upon him (1 Sam 16:23). With great narrative irony, David is the cause of both Saul's trouble and Saul's relief. The movement of the spirit onto David was the cause of the evil spirit coming upon Saul (16:13–14) and now David's music is the cause of his relief and the departure of that evil spirit from him. David has thus far in the narrative been completely passive. He has not spoken and he has mostly been moved around. Saul, on the other hand, has been active and is the cause of David entering his service. However, David is the active cause of both the good and the bad that comes to a passive Saul who cannot seem to do anything about it. The theme of David as the active one and Saul as the passive one will continue in the next chapter.

DAVID AND THE GIANT(S) (1 SAMUEL 17)

The story of David and Goliath is certainly one of the most iconic in all the Bible. It has been depicted and represented in countless different ways. It is the subject of high art such as the trilogy of paintings by Caravaggio. It is the subject of children's entertainment, such as the video series VeggieTales where David is depicted as an asparagus and Goliath as a giant pickle. It is a scene that has captured the imagination of readers for millennia and it is the story that catapults David to stardom, both in the context of his story and in the context of interpretive history. It is a scene that has been studied and studied and studied again.[10] As such we will

---

10. I myself have written about it several times. See Johnson, "Did David Bring a Gun to a Knife Fight?"; Johnson, *Reading David and Goliath in Greek and Hebrew*; and Johnson, "Making a First Impression."

not be able to say everything there is to say about this justly famous scene. We will, however, attempt to make a few relevant comments that help to appreciate the importance of this scene for understanding who David is.

Setting the Scene (1 Samuel 17:1–11)

The scene begins with a detailed description of the geography of the confrontation. In the first three verses, five different place names are listed (Socoh, Judah, Azekah, Ephes-Damim, valley of Elah) and a detailed picture of the landscape is painted:

> The Philistines stood on the mountain on the one side, and Israel stood on the mountain on the other side, with a valley between them.
> (1 Sam 17:3)

The place names situate the confrontation as a Philistine incursion into the Elah Valley, a place that is significant economically and militarily. This region could be described as a gateway between Philistine territory and Israelite/Judahite territory. The physical setting paints the scene. One gets the sense that we are looking at an arena. All eyes are on the valley between the two armies, expecting the action that will follow.

The next thing that happens is the introduction of the Philistine champion, who is given a detailed description that is unrivaled in biblical narrative. He is described as armored from head to toe. In modern terms, he is described as a tank.[11] As sparse as biblical narrative is in describing

---

11. There is a lot of literature on Goliath's armor. Some suggest that his armor does not reflect an appropriate picture of an iron-age warrior. Others think that the descriptions of his armor are not far removed from the depiction of twelfth century Mycenean warriors, which would be appropriate for the setting in the David and Goliath

the physical features of its characters, we, the readers, are forced to spend four verses staring at Goliath. The effect on the reader is probably intended to be the same as the effect on the Israelites: awe and fear.

Goliath immediately offers a challenge of mockery that is fitting to this kind of military confrontation. It might look to modern readers a little bit like trash talking, because that is exactly what it is. He taunts Israel and challenges them to one-on-one combat, known throughout the ancient Near East and especially in the Greek tradition as *monomachia* ("single combat").[12] Modern readers should be familiar with this scenario from the opening scene of the 2004 film *Troy*. The opening scene of that movie sees Brad Pitt's Achilles facing off against Boagrius, the giant champion of Thessaly. Poor Boagrius.

The response of Saul and the people is one of dismay and great fear (1 Sam 17:11). The scene is set. There is a significant military incursion by the enemies of the people of Israel. The setting is an arena, not unlike a gladiatorial colosseum. A giant and tank-like champion has thrown down the gauntlet and challenged the people of Israel. The moment is set for a hero. Now is the time for a king who is supposed to fight the people's battles (see 1 Sam 8:19–20). Saul, while not hiding among the baggage, is, however, hiding among the people "dismayed and greatly afraid" (1 Sam 17:11), but like 80s pop singer Bonnie Tyler, we need a hero. Cue the music.

---

story. For two recent examples following that line, see King, "David Defeats Goliath"; and Millard, "The Armor of Goliath."

12. See Esler, "Ancient Mediterranean Monomachia."

A Shepherd Boy's Quest (1 Samuel 17:12–31)

With the game on the line and Israel and their king quaking in fear, the scene now changes to re-introduce us to David. The wording of verse 12 feels like an introduction to a new character: "Now David was the son of an Ephrathite..." (cf. Saul's introduction in 1 Sam 9:1). For that reason, this scene is often thought of as another introduction to David.

In *this* introduction, David, the youngest son, is sent on a quest to bring provisions to his brothers, who were serving in Saul's military (17:17–18). Quickly and easily completing his quest (contra to Saul, who couldn't complete the quest his father sent him on in chapter 9), David just happens to arrive at the time that Goliath came out and gave his daily challenge (17:23). David's response is important. Robert Alter, an important literary critic of the Hebrew Bible, has commented that in biblical narrative a character's first words are often "a defining moment of characterization."[13] David's first words will prove that to be true.[14]

> "What shall be done for the man who kills this Philistine, and takes away the reproach from Israel? For who is this uncircumcised Philistine that he should defy the armies of the living God?"
>
> (1 Sam 17:26)

It is possible to see David's first words as primarily self-serving words about personal gain. That is true of the first question in David's first words. However, it is also possible to put the emphasis on the second question, which is much more theologically astute and shows David recognizing the

---

13. Alter, *The David Story*, 105.
14. For further reflection on this see Johnson, "Making a First Impression."

theological problem of Goliath's challenge. It seems the best way to understand this defining moment of characterization is to see that David does in fact say two things: one that seems concerned for his reward and one that seems concerned for God's reputation. This is entirely fitting, given the complexity of David's characterization, which we will see throughout his story. David is one who is ambitious and opportunistic, but that does not mean that he is not also theologically aware and concerned for God's reputation. He is *both* of those things.

It is also worth briefly noting that David's first words earn him a sharp rebuke from his older brother, Eliab, who claims that he *knows* the evil of David's *heart* (17:28). We have already seen the significance of heart language, but we will see the significance of "knowing" soon. Now, we must ask whether Eliab is here just being a jealous older brother or if he has some insight into David's character. We have just had a positive judgment of David's heart from God (16:7), so we know that Eliab is not entirely correct in his assessment of David. However, the fact is that Eliab at least causes us to question whether we really know what is in David's heart. After all, the point that God made is that only God has access to the hearts of human beings. So the point still stands, even as much as we currently know about David, we do not fully know what is in his heart. We are left to continue to consider that question.

David responds to Eliab's rebuke by asking the rhetorical question, "What have I done now?" (1 Sam 17:29). The answer to that question is: nothing . . . yet.

David vs. the (Israelite) Giant (1 Samuel 17:32–40)

Having spoken his daring first words, the men of the camp bring him before Saul and David utters another significant

Making a First Impression

phrase, this time before the king. He says: "Let no one's heart fail because of him; your servant will go and fight with this Philistine" (17:32).[15] Here we have the key theme of the heart coming to the fore. Though David says, "let no one's heart fail," that is precisely what has happened. The hearts of Saul and the Israelites have failed because of the Philistine giant. By implication we learn that David has a heart that will not fail.

Saul, understandably, does not think that David has a chance of defeating the Philistine champion. David, on the other hand, is prepared to make his case and offers to Saul what is sometimes called "David's boast" (17:34–37). In this boast to Saul he details his exploits as a surprisingly militant shepherd. Among the significant things to note in David's boast is the reason he claims he will be successful against the Philistine champion. In response to Saul's claim that David will not be able to face the Philistine giant, David details what would happen whenever a lion or bear would take a lamb from the flock. He would go after it, strike it down, and save the lamb (1 Sam 17:35–36). He claims that, because he has personally faced lions and bears, he is capable of fighting giants, whether four-legged or otherwise, so he will be able to fight the Philistine giant. However, he immediately reinterprets his success in his next statement,

> "The LORD, who saved me from the paw of the
> lion and from the paw of the bear, will save me
> from the hand of this Philistine."
>
> (1 Sam 17:37)

So, which is it? Is David capable of fighting off the giant because he is a skilled fighter, capable of facing lions and bears? Or, is it that *God* will deliver David from the

---

15. Interestingly, the Greek text here reads "Let not *my lord's* heart fail," which draws a greater contrast between David, whose heart will not fail, and Saul, whose heart apparently is failing.

Philistine enemy the way that he has delivered David from his beastly enemies? It seems that David's answer leads us to conclude that David, at least, thinks that it is both. David has blended his actions with God's actions. This seems like an example of what biblical scholars call *dual causality*.[16] The basic idea is that the biblical authors write in such a way as sometimes to attribute causality both to God and humans. This seems to be what David is doing here. He is attributing his success against lions and bears to his own actions. He is then immediately attributing that success to God. But which is it? How are we to understand this? The biblical narrative simply holds up the cause as human and divine and leaves it at that, to the frustration of many theological systems. Then again, the advantage in telling a story, as opposed to offering a theological argument, is that such ambiguity can stand.

Whatever the cause, Saul accepts David's rationale and allows him to go forth and fight the Philistine champion. However, before he lets David take off to fight the giant, he decides to armor the young shepherd. David, of course, refuses Saul's armor (17:38–39a). Despite the tendency to view this as a comedic moment where a giant king is arming a little boy, the point of this scene is to give David an opportunity symbolically to reject Saul's way of facing the conflict. For, as we will soon learn, one point of this conflict is to show that God does not save by conventional warfare.

Having rejected Saul's armor, he takes his staff in hand and chooses five smooth stones for his sling and heads to face the Philistine champion (17:40). There is a tendency to misinterpret David's use of a sling. David's sling is neither a child's toy like a Dennis-the-Menace style slingshot, nor is it the equivalent of bringing a gun to a knife fight in the style

---

16. On this phenomenon see Amit, "The Dual Causality Principle."

of Indiana Jones.[17] Rather, the sling was an effective ancient weapon. However, it was most often used in big groups to barrage the enemy with stone after stone after stone. It was occasionally used by specialist fighters (cf. Judg 20:16). However, David's use of the sling in *this instance*, against a heavily armored fighter, is a one in a million shot. Or, as I have elsewhere argued,

> a modern analogy to David's victory over Goliath is Luke Skywalker's victory over the Death Star in George Lucas's *Star Wars*. While it may be physically possible for a proton torpedo to penetrate a small thermal exhaust port on the Death Star, it is highly unlikely and the viewer knows the real secret to Luke's success. Similarly, while it may be physically possible for David to take down the well-armored Goliath with a sling, it is highly unlikely and the reader knows the real secret to David's success. In short, just as the Force was with Luke, [God] was with David.[18]

Facing the (Philistine) Giant (1 Samuel 17:41–54)

Once David is finally facing Goliath, we still do not get the actual contest. Instead, we get more words. In fact, in this lengthy chapter known as the battle of David and Goliath, only three verses are dedicated to the actual combat. A substantial amount of the rest of the chapter is dedicated to dialogue. It is almost as if the words *about* the conflict are more important than the conflict itself.

---

17. For discussion of the effectiveness of the sling, see Johnson, "Did David Bring a Gun to a Knife Fight?"

18. Johnson, "Did David Bring a Gun to a Knife Fight?" 537.

Goliath is incensed at seeing David (17:42). It is perhaps interesting to reflect on the fact that after spending a chapter where *seeing* David was thematic and surprising, we now are told that the Philistine champion was also surprised upon *seeing* David. Immediately, we are back to Goliath's taunt from earlier in the chapter and are in the midst of ancient Near Eastern trash talk. Goliath picks up right where he left off, cursing David by his gods and telling David how he will feed his flesh to wild animals (17:43–44). David, not to be outdone, turns out to be a champion trash talker. He claims that Goliath's sword and spear will be no match for the God of Israel, who will deliver David. As fantastic as all of this trash talking rhetoric is, the most important part of this dialogue, and arguably the most important part of the whole chapter, is David's stated reasons for his upcoming victory.

> "This very day the LORD will deliver you into my hand, and I will strike you down and cut off your head ... *so that* all the earth may know that there is a God in Israel, and *that* all this assembly may know that the LORD does not save by sword and spear; for the battle is the LORD's."
>
> (1 Sam 17:46–47)

Here we come to the theological heart of this narrative. According to David, the reason that God is going to give him victory is in order to teach two related but different theological lessons. First, David says that his victory will teach all the earth that there is a God in Israel. This suggests that David's victory will be testimony to the presence of God in Israel throughout the world. Second, David says that *this assembly* (probably referring to Israel) will know that God does not save by sword and spear. The fact that God does not save by sword and spear is a significant theological lesson that Israel needs to learn. After all, they requested a king in the first place so that they could be *like other nations* (1 Sam 8:20). The king that they were given looks exactly like what one would expect given those conventional expectations. According to David, however, Israel needs to learn a lesson that God is not dependent upon conventional warfare and Israel is not meant to be either.

Having exchanged wit and words, the combatants now turn to exchanging weapons and wounds. The action happens quickly. Verse 49 is almost all verbs. David rushes toward Goliath takes out his stone, slings it, and strikes the Philistine, who falls face down. The careful reader may note that just as Goliath's god, Dagon, fell face first before the ark of the Lord in 1 Sam 5:3–4, Goliath now falls face first before the chosen one of the Lord. David, true to his word, cuts off Goliath's head with his own sword.

The sight of their fallen champion leads the Philistines to dismay and the route begins (17:51a–52). Significantly, the narrative ends where it began, with geography. Just as the narrative began with reference to the geography of the confrontation in order to signal the Philistine incursion, the narrative now ends with reference to the geographical extent of the Philistine flight to signal Israel's total victory (17:52–53).

Introducing David . . . Yet Again? (1 Samuel 17:55–58)

The David and Goliath episode ends with a curious scene. After the narration of the victory, the reader is taken, in a flashback, to the moment that David goes out to face the giant. We see that moment from Saul's perspective. Seeing David head out to face the giant, Saul turns to Abner, his general, and asks, "whose son is this young man?" (1 Sam 17:55). Abner apparently does not know. How can this be? We know that David had entered Saul's court as a musician and armor bearer (1 Sam 16:21–23; 17:15). Are Saul and Abner suffering from amnesia? There are a number of ways to wrestle with this apparent difficulty, including noting that here Saul is specifically asking about the identity of David's father, but I think we might lose the point of this scene by focusing on this difficulty. When we were first introduced to David, we were introduced to the idea that only God can see into the interior of a person (1 Sam 16:7). When David first shows up on the scene as a character, his brother causes us to question whether or not we know what is in David's heart (1 Sam 17:28). Now, at the conclusion of David's great moment we are presented with a scene, which three times asks the question of whose son David is (17:55–58) and the only response is that he is the son of Jesse the Bethlehemite (17:58). We are given no new information, though we are forced to focus on the question of David's identity. I can't help but wonder if this scene is included to force us once again to ask the question about David's identity without answering it. We are not God, we don't have a privileged perspective into David's identity. We can only see his actions and hear his words and we must make judgments accordingly. For the rest of this story we will be asking this question about who David really is and it seems significant that we are forced to ask it three times immediately after David's initial entrance into the narrative.

CONCLUSION: OUR FIRST IMPRESSIONS OF DAVID

We have spent considerably more time on these first two chapters than we will be able to do with any other part of David's story. Even this rather lengthy chapter, however, feels woefully inadequate to unpack the significance of our introduction to David in 1 Samuel 16–17. Hopefully, we

Making a First Impression

have unpacked enough to get a sense of the first impression that David makes when he arrives on the scene of the biblical narrative. We have spent quite a bit of time *seeing* David. What have we seen?

We have seen a man who, though he may not fit the standard categories of an ancient Near Eastern warlord, is a man whose heart is judged positively by God (16:1–13), though we know we can never fully penetrate what is in his heart. We have seen a man who has an impressive resumé that hints at the future legacy that he will have (16:14–23). We have seen a young warrior who is marked both by ambition and by faith (17:26). We have seen a man whose heart will not fail him even when the hearts of everyone around him fail (17:32). We have seen a man who understands that there is blending between his actions and God's (17:34–37). We have seen a man that understands the missional significance of this conflict as his victory will communicate something about God's presence in Israel to the rest of the world (17:46). We have seen a man that recognizes that his people need to learn a lesson about dependence upon God (17:47). Finally, we have seen a man who is willing to put himself at great risk and face the enemies of God by putting his trust in God (17:48–51).

These opening chapters have also caused us to see that there will always be questions about David's identity. This was especially the case in Eliab's accusations (17:28) and Saul's questions (17:55–58). These opening chapters have also already shown us the complex characterization of David as one who has multiple sides and motivations. However, it has also shown us that he is clearly God's chosen leader who trusts God and enjoys a special kind of relationship with him. This final fact will be perhaps the most significant thing about David and what is true about our first impression of him will continue to be true throughout his story even as David's characterization continues to get more and more complex.

QUESTIONS FOR REFLECTION

1. What do you think is the significance of David's detailed physical description?
2. How do you interpret the emphasis of David's first words? Do they seem primarily self-serving or are they primarily about David's faith?
3. What do you make of these apparent multiple introductions to David? Why do you think we seem to have multiple introductions to him?
4. David sees his actions and God's actions overlapping. To what extent are we permitted to see overlap between our actions and God's actions today?

3

ROYAL RELATIONSHIPS
1 Samuel 18–20

> [T]he soul of Jonathan was bound to the soul of David, and Jonathan loved him as his own soul.
>
> Now Saul's daughter Michal loved David.
>
> Saul was still more afraid of David. So Saul was David's enemy from that time forward.
>
> —Narrator[1]

IN THE 2004 FILM, *Meet the Parents*, Ben Stiller's character, Greg Focker, has to survive a weekend with his future in-laws. The humor in the film is derived from the fact that Ben Stiller's character could not have worse interactions with his father-in-law, who, it turns out is a former CIA agent. We cannot help but feel sympathy for Stiller's character, even as we laugh at the hilarity of his horrible

---

1. 1 Sam 18:1, 20, 29.

situation as he accidentally floods the septic tank, accidentally bloodies the nose of his future sister-in-law, and much more. However, as bad as things go for poor Greg Focker, at least his father-in-law does not repeatedly try to kill him. The same cannot be said for David and his interactions with his father-in-law, Saul.

In the previous chapter we saw David come on the scene. His victory over the Philistine giant catapults him into prominence. The collection of scenes that we will look at in this chapter will pick up where the last chapter left off and see David's interactions with the royal family as a result of his victory over Goliath.

DAVID'S SUCCESS AND SAUL'S DAUGHTERS (1 SAMUEL 18)

Chapter 18 picks up immediately where chapter 17 left off. After David finishes speaking to Saul at the battlefield, we read the following.

> When David had finished speaking to Saul, the soul of Jonathan was bound to the soul of David, and Jonathan loved him as his own soul. ... Then Jonathan made a covenant with David, because he loved him as his own soul. Jonathan stripped himself of the robe that he was wearing, and gave it to David, and his armor, and even his sword and his bow and his belt.
>
> (1 Sam 18:1–4)

Understanding the David and Jonathan relationship is crucial for David's characterization, since it is arguably his closest and most important relationship early in his life. Here we see the beginning of this relationship and a few things stand out. First, we note the personal, intimate, and emotional aspect of his relationship in the phrase "the soul of Jonathan was bound to the soul of David" (1 Sam 18:1). There are a lot of different interpretations of this phrase about David and Jonathan and we will address some of it in the Excursus below. At the very least, this language suggests a level of special familial intimacy (cf. Jacob's feelings about his son Benjamin in Gen 44:30).

The second significance in David and Jonathan's initial meeting is the language of love that characterizes this relationship. Again, this language is sometimes misunderstood. It is true that love language in the Bible can mean emotional love, the way that we use word today (see esp. Michal in 1 Sam 18:20 and the Song of Songs). However, in the Old Testament, love language most frequently suggests something more akin to dedication and loyalty, sometimes even political loyalty (cf. Deut 10:12–13). Thus, the language of love is meant to suggest obedience and loyalty more than a feeling. It is frequently about total commitment. It does not necessarily deny emotional content, neither does it require it.

A third key aspect of this interaction is that David and Jonathan make an official covenant here. We are not told any specifics of this covenant, but it is important that David and Jonathan have made their relationship a covenantal one. This theme will be sounded again.

A final significance of David and Jonathan's first exchange is Jonathan's gift of clothing to David (18:4). We previously remarked about the symbolic importance of David refusing Saul's armor and how it likely represented David's refusal of Saul's way of kingship. Now, in this significant meeting between David and Saul's oldest son, we cannot help but see some significance in Jonathan giving David his robe, his armor, his belt, his sword, and especially his bow. The general gifting of his clothes and armaments seems to signal that this act of giving David his robe and his armaments marks Jonathan's recognition that David now functions as Saul's rightful heir to the throne.[2] The beginning of David and Jonathan's relationship, therefore, is marked by personal commitment, formal commitment, and a recognition by Jonathan that David is the future.

We move from the beginning of the David and Jonathan relationship to learn more about David's early life in Saul's court. Saul's first response to David was a positive reception (16:21). After David's victory over Goliath, however, it is clear that Saul now sees him as a rival and a threat (see 18:9, 12). It is perhaps easy to accuse Saul of being paranoid, especially since the text is going to continue to remind us that David is not trying to steal the throne. However, his response seems to be a natural human reaction to a competitor. David is Mozart to Saul's Salieri. David's ascent may be inevitable, but, probably, so is Saul's envy.

With the rivalry between David and Saul now established, we now see one of Saul's early attempts to get rid of David in his offer of marriage to his daughters. The arrangement with his eldest daughter, Merab, does not work out. David seems to decline the offer and Saul gives Merab to another (18:18–19). Things change when Saul learns that his daughter Michal loves David. He sees in this fact another opportunity against David (18:20–21). Apparently, Saul is not opposed to using his daughters as pawns in his game against David. He offers David his second daughter and sets the bride price at one hundred Philistine foreskins, thinking that David will get killed attempting to fulfill it (18:25).

Saul's plan backfires. Instead of resulting in David's death, Saul's plan leads to more success for David as he easily procures one hundred (or perhaps two hundred)

---

2. Cf. Firth, *1 & 2 Samuel*, 208.

Royal Relationships

Philistine foreskins (18:26–27).[3] His daughter Michal loves David and is married to him, and David's fame continues to rise (18:28–30).

We actually learn more about Saul's characterization in this chapter than David's. As Robert Alter once remarked, throughout the first part of David's story, he remains somewhat opaque.[4] We get plenty of insight into Saul's psyche, mostly his growing paranoia about David, but we get very little information about how David feels about any of the situations that we find him in. Even the note that he was pleased to marry Michal, actually says that he was "pleased to be the king's son-in-law" (18:26). Is that due to his feelings for Michal or his desire to gain status in Israel? We are not told. We have been led to ask the question: "who is David?" But we have yet to be given very many answers.

PROTECTING DAVID (1 SAMUEL 19)

Chapter 19 continues to narrate the tension between David and Saul, but focuses significantly on David's relationships with Saul's children, Jonathan and Michal.

Initially, Saul includes Jonathan in his plots to kill David (19:1). Jonathan's loyalties, however, clearly lie with David. Jonathan keeps David informed about his father's murderous intent and lobbies his father on David's behalf (19:2–5). His argument is that David has been a great asset to Saul and to Israel. Specifically, he references David's victory over Goliath. Jonathan reminds Saul that he rejoiced at David's victory over the Philistine champion (19:4). Why then would Saul seek to kill David? It appears that Jonathan

---

3. The NRSV reads "one hundred" based on the Greek. The Hebrew and most translations read "two hundred" (NIV, NASB, ESV, JPS).

4. Alter, *The Art of Biblical Narrative*, 152.

would have a successful career in Washington D.C., because his lobbying works and Saul relents his desire to kill David, at least for now. Jonathan manages to work out a temporary reconciliation between David and Saul (19:7).

The reconciliation does not last long, however. Saul is once again haunted by an evil spirit from the LORD and attempts to spear David to the wall, but David escapes (19:10). David has been and will continue to receive help from Saul's children, but in this instance, David appears to save himself with his own resourcefulness.

David apparently goes home because Saul immediately sends messengers to David's house to keep watch until morning when they are to kill him. Somehow Michal finds out about this and warns David and helps him escape out the window (19:11–12). In order to cover up David's escape, Michal places a household idol (*teraphim*) in David's bed and disguises it to look like him. The reference to the rarely mentioned household idol characterizes Michal as a new Rachel, who also deceived her deceiving father with the use of "household idols" (*teraphim*, Gen 31:19–35).[5] Saul, however, is potentially characterized a little more negatively here. It is worth recalling that when Samuel chastised Saul for not obeying God's command, he said "stubbornness is like iniquity and *idolatry*" (Heb. *teraphim*, 1 Sam 15:23), thus it may be that the picture here of a household idol (Heb. *teraphim*) standing in for David is meant to convey the idea that Saul's idol is David, or rather catching David.[6] Thus, Michal, a new Rachel, helps David escape Saul, who has become obsessed with him.

David flees to Samuel at Ramah. Perhaps David sees that it was Samuel who got him into this mess in the first

---

5. On this view see Firth, *1 & 2 Samuel*, 217–18, and Bodner and White, "Some Advantages of Recycling."

6. See Chapman, *1 Samuel*, 165–66.

place. Or, perhaps David recognizes that Samuel is the only other figure in Israel that could possibly stand up to Saul. Saul sends men to take David, but a curious thing happens. Every time Saul's men approach Samuel and his band of prophets, they fall into a prophetic frenzy. This presumably involves some kind of raving activity, whether or not that included glow sticks, laser lights, or electronic DJ music. Whatever is involved, it renders them incapacitated and they cannot take David. This happens to two different sets of Saul's messengers, before Saul decides that if you want something done right you've got to do it yourself. Saul, too joins the rave, leading to the proverb, "Is Saul also among the prophets?" (19:24). This phrase was originally applied to Saul when his prophetic activity was a sign that the LORD was with him (1 Sam 10:6, 10–12). This second time that the spirit leads Saul into a prophetic frenzy it is a sign that the LORD is not with him but with David. The spirit that initially worked with him is now working against him. So David has been protected by Jonathan, Michal, and now by Samuel. Saul, it ought to be fair to say, must feel that everyone is against him, including the spirit of the LORD.

JONATHAN AND DAVID (1 SAMUEL 20)

David continues to be on the run and he comes before Jonathan.

> "What have I done? What is my guilt? And what is my sin against your father that he is trying to take my life?"
>
> (1 Sam 20:1)

David's questions here are somewhat provocative. We have already noted David's propensity for asking questions about himself (cf. 1 Sam 17:26), including this exact question, "what have I done now?" (1 Sam 17:29). He is clearly showing a defensive posture and the implied answer to these questions is, nothing. However, it adds to the tension about David's identity. David might not quite be Forky from *Toy Story 4*, constantly asking why he is alive, but he seems to ask a lot of questions about his identity, and we, the readers, can't help doing so as well.

Jonathan tells David that he has nothing to worry about because Saul trusts Jonathan with everything and Jonathan will act as a spy for David (20:2). David, however, is not so sure and tells Jonathan that he fears for his life (20:3). What we get here is a brief insight into David's mental state. It seems that he truly perceives that his life hangs in the balance and he is one misstep away from Saul getting exactly what he wants, namely, David's demise.

Jonathan agrees to be a spy for David in Saul's court and the two friends make another covenant of loyalty with each other. This time the focus is on Jonathan's descendants. He makes David swear to "never cut off your faithful love from my house" (20:15). Essentially, Jonathan is ensuring that David will show loyalty to his children if Jonathan ends up dead when David takes the throne. An ominous foreshadowing of what will eventually occur. It is perhaps significant, however, in this section that focuses on the growing tension between David and Saul, that it is framed by the covenant commitment of David and Jonathan (1 Sam 18:3 and 20:14–17).[7]

When Saul shows his anger at David because he is not present at a new moon meal, it becomes clear to Jonathan that Saul meant to kill David all along. Saul, for his part lashes out against Jonathan. In his lashing out against Jonathan, not only does Saul seem to hurl intense insults at him,

---

7. Firth, *1 & 2 Samuel*, 223.

but he eventually hurls his spear at him as well (20:33).[8] This episode shows that Saul has clearly slipped into full-blown paranoia. What started as suspicion against his servant David (18:9) has become homicidal rage against his own son![9]

After Saul has made his point (literally!), that he is an enemy of David and that this will not change, Jonathan signals to David and David comes to Jonathan for their last farewell. The farewell is clearly intimate and emotional (20:41).[10] Perhaps the most important piece of information here is given in the final phrase of this verse, "David wept the more" (20:41).[11] We have been noting along the way that we know many characters' perspectives toward David, but we are yet to see David's inner thoughts or feelings. We know that Saul probably loved him initially (16:21), Jonathan loved him (18:1, 3), Michal loved him (18:20, 28), and all Israel and Judah loved him (18:16). We even know that God judges him positively (13:14, 16:7, 12). Now, we get our first insight into David's thoughts or feelings and perhaps surprisingly, they are extreme and even surpass Jonathan's!

This is a significant moment for our understanding of the characterization of David. Though there has been little insight into David's character, we now see into his heart and

8. For a brief but helpful discussion of the possible ways to interpret the phrase, "You son of a perverse, rebellious woman" and "the shame of your mother's nakedness," see Chapman, *1 Samuel*, 170, n. 144. However we interpret Saul's language, it is clearly very harsh and emotive.

9. For an excellent study of Saul that suggests that his behavior is similar to that of an addict, see Evans, "From a Head above the Rest to No Head at All."

10. On the possible sexual connotations of this act, see the Excursus below.

11. This phrase is actually a little textually difficult. However, most commentators take it to mean that David's weeping surpassed Jonathan's, hence the NRSV's translation. For helpful discussion see Smith, *Poetic Heroes*, 66 and 401 n. 126.

see his love for Jonathan and the sorrow at parting from his friend. Why are we only seeing this now? Perhaps it was important for David to remain somewhat opaque up to this point, so that the reader gets used to asking questions about David's character. Perhaps it is significant that we most frequently see insight into David's character in extreme situations, such as here. Other places include the death of Jonathan (2 Sam 1:26), the mortal illness of his newborn son with Bathsheba (2 Sam 12:12:16–18), and the death of Absalom (2 Sam 19:4). Perhaps these extreme moments in David's life show us that although we do not always have insight into David's motivations and feelings, there are intense things going on inside David, they are just below the surface and out of sight. After all, it is only God who can look into the human heart (16:7).

CONCLUSION

In this chapter we have looked at David's time in the court of Saul. We have seen his relationships with the royal family. A few things seem entirely clear. First, throughout this part of the story, Saul can do no right and David can do no wrong. Every attempt Saul makes on David's life only increases David's success and fame or pushes Saul's own children further into David's camp. Second, and related to the first, is the fact that the LORD is now with David and he is not with Saul. The narrative has explicitly confirmed this at times, but more often, the narrative fact of David's successes and Saul's failures seem to be confirmation. Third, David has garnered the loyalty of Saul's two named children, Jonathan and Michal. Finally, David has largely remained mysterious. We have seen little insight into his psyche. In this portion of the narrative we have mostly seen him profess his innocence, kill Philistines, and evade Saul. However, in the end, we saw the intensity of his emotions and his love for Jonathan. So we are perhaps justified in thinking that like the Transformer toys of my childhood, with David there is more than meets the eye!

EXCURSUS: THE RELATIONSHIP OF DAVID AND JONATHAN

Since we have spent some time reflecting on the relationship between David and Jonathan in this chapter, it is probably beneficial to reflect a little bit on the nature of that relationship. It is not uncommon today to see David and Jonathan as an ancient example of a homosexual relationship. A few different perspectives can be given to show the various ways that this relationship has been interpreted.

> David and Jonathan shared a homoerotic and, more than likely, a homosexual relationship. The books of Samuel recount the love of the two men with utter frankness.[12]

> A sexual dimension in the relationship between David and Jonathan can only be claimed if the biblical descriptions of this relationship are not taken at face value, but expanded by having recourse to a presumed hidden message.[13]

What are we to make of this? It will not do to deny that the description of David and Jonathan's relationship does not contain substantial intimate and even potentially sexually charged language. However, it needs to be asked whether that language actually implies a sexual relationship. Let's

---

12. Schroer and Staubli, "Saul, David, and Jonathan," 22.
13. Zehnder, "Observations on the Relationship between David and Jonathan," 174.

take a brief look at some of the descriptions of David and Jonathan's relationship that may imply something sexual.

First, upon their first meeting it is said that "the soul of Jonathan was bound to the soul of David, and Jonathan loved him as his own soul" (18:1). We have already commented on "love" language in the Bible and noted that it does not predominantly imply emotion, but rather commitment, being frequently associated with covenant. The language of one's soul being bound to another is used elsewhere in the Bible to describe the special connection between Jacob and his youngest son Benjamin (Gen 44:30). Thus, while intimacy and a special, perhaps familial, relationship is surely implied, a sexual aspect of that relationship need not be, and a bond between a father and a beloved son may be more what is in mind here.

Second, the David and Jonathan relationship is certainly full of emotional language. Jonathan is said to take great delight in David (19:1). It is said that Jonathan "likes" David (20:3 NRSV), or better, David has "found favor" in Jonathan's eyes (20:3, NIV, NASB, ESV). Jonathan is also said, not just to love David, but to love him as his own life or soul (18:1; 20:17). Furthermore, at Jonathan and David's parting we see both of them weeping (20:41). There can be no doubt that there is a strong emotional connection between David and Jonathan. In fact, it is also clear that the narrative makes the emotional connection between David and Jonathan more emphatic than probably any other relationship, much more so than with David and any of his wives. We will need to ask why that is, but we will simply note it for now.

Third, there is evidence of physical displays of emotion in David and Jonathan's relationship. In their parting it is described that David "bowed three times, and they kissed each other, and wept with each other; David wept the more"

(20:41). While in modern western culture a kiss generally only has a sexual or romantic connotation, that is not the case in all cultures and has not been the case through time. In this context, it seems much more likely to convey familial intimacy and imply that David and Jonathan view each other as brothers.[14]

Finally, in David's lament for Jonathan, we see the famous statement:

> "I am distressed for you, my brother Jonathan; greatly beloved were you to me; your love to me was wonderful, passing the love of women."
>
> (2 Sam 1:26)

This statement has garnered a lot of attention and has at times been seen as evidence for a homosexual relationship between David and Jonathan.[15] However, it less than clear that that is what this language implies. First of all, the reference to the love of women in this statement is a comparative, not necessarily of kind, but of degree. The point of the language of "passing the love of women" is that David is describing his relationship with Jonathan in terms that surpasses the most intimate relationship that he can point to, a marital relationship. It need not imply that it is comparing the kind of relationship implied by a marital relationship, namely, a sexually intimate one. Second of all, as Susan Ackerman points out, given the general condemnation of male-male sexual relationships in the Old Testament, it seems hard to argue for a positively assessed one here.[16]

---

14. For a survey of references to kissing in the Old Testament, see Zehnder, "Observations on the Relationship between David and Jonathan," 149–50. For some discussion of the significance of kissing in the ancient Near East, see Smith, *Poetic Heroes*, 86–87. Cf. similarly, Ackerman, *When Heroes Love*, 67.

15. See for example, Olyan, "Surpassing the Love of Women."

16. Ackerman, *When Heroes Love*, 198.

DAVID

Finally, a very appropriate contemporary example of this can be given. In honor of the 75th anniversary of D-Day, the BBC aired an interview with a veteran of the Normandy invasion, Harry Billinge. In his reminiscence of that event he had the following to say.

> Normandy veterans love one another beyond the love of women. If you was in a hole in the ground with a bloke, you got to know him. Marvelous men. My generation saved the world and I'll never forget any of them.[17]

The interviewer, Naga Munchetty, was clearly moved by this exchange and rightly so. It would be inappropriate and disrespectful to imply that this statement by a Normandy veteran had anything to do with homosexuality. It is simply a statement by a military hero who is celebrating the men that fought and died with him. He is testifying about the clearly non-sexual intimacy of military men who go through an experience like the Normandy invasion together.

So with that, why is there this emotionally charged language at all in the David and Jonathan relationship? I think the above quote by Harry Billinge gives a clue. The relationship of military men has the capacity to be intensely intimate. In the case of David and Jonathan, who are depicted as a warrior pair like we see elsewhere in the ancient Near East, this kind of intimacy is understandable. As Mark Smith has argued, this kind of seemingly sexually charged, intimate, and even physical description of the relationship between warrior pairs is to be expected, but not because these relationships were understood to be homosexual relationships. Rather, the intimate and physical nature of

---

17. Interview with WWII veteran, Harry Billinge on BBC Breakfast. 6 June 2019. BBC: https://www.bbc.com/news/av/uk-48543293/d-day-veteran-harry-billinge-i-m-no-hero-i-was-lucky. Accessed 21 June 2019.

the bonds formed by warriors together lends itself toward language that is drawn from male-female intimate relationships. This stresses both the degree of intimacy formed by these warriors and even the physical intimacy gained in battle.[18] This is a much more plausible explanation for the kinds of descriptions that we see in the David–Jonathan relationship than the suggestion that we are meant to see them as having a homosexual relationship. The David-Jonathan relationship probably does not provide support for or condemnation of homosexual relationships. Rather the question of homosexuality does not appear to feature in the David-Jonathan relationship. That this is a prominent question for modern readers likely highlights the cultural distance between our contemporary culture and the culture of the Old Testament.

QUESTIONS FOR REFLECTION

1. Why do you think we get limited access to David's inner life, his thoughts, or feelings?
2. How would you describe David in this portion of the narrative? What characteristics stand out?
3. What do you make of the different kinds of relationships that David has with Saul, Jonathan, and Michal?
4. What do you take away from the description of the David and Jonathan relationship?

---

18. Smith, *Poetic Heroes*, 92–93, writes, "The claim that I want to explore is this: on the physical level, conflict shared by warrior males is like sexual relations shared between men and women. Both, in a sense, involve clashes of bodies: women and men with one another in sexual relations, heroes together in physical combat at each other's side."

4

RUN, DAVID! RUN!
1 Samuel 21–26

"Who among all your servants is so faithful as David? He is the king's son-in-law, and is quick to do your bidding, and is honored in your house"
—Ahimelech[1]

"Who is David? Who is the son of Jesse?"
—Nabal[2]

You are more righteous than I; for you have repaid me good, whereas I have repaid you evil.
—Saul[3]

IN THE NOW CLASSIC 1994 film, *Forrest Gump*, we are introduced to a young boy named Forrest Gump who has a back

1. 1 Sam 22:14.
2. 1 Sam 25:10.
3. 1 Sam 24:17.

problem that requires him to wear very prominent braces on his legs. He speaks a little differently and he is not the smartest in his class. When you add leg braces to that, it is not surprising that he is bullied in school. In one iconic scene, Forrest is attacked by a bunch of bullies. While his sweetheart, Jenny Curran, cheers him on, "Run, Forrest! Run!" Forrest takes off. At first, he runs awkwardly in his leg braces. But soon, as the bullies bear down on him, his stride starts to normalize, his braces break off his legs, and he discovers, as he says in the film, that he can run like the wind blows! It takes bullies chasing him for him to discover his ability as a runner.

In this portion of David's story, he is also on the run. We will see whether or not he discovers anything about himself in the process.

DAVID ELUDES SAUL (1 SAMUEL 21–23)

David, Saul, and the Events at Nob (1 Samuel 21–22)

With David now officially on the run from Saul, his first stop is with the priest Ahimelech at Nob. It is interesting that Ahimelech comes "trembling" to meet David (1 Sam 21:1). This is the exact same posture in which the elders of Bethlehem come to greet Samuel when he arrives to anoint David in the first place (see 1 Sam 16:1). Are we being reminded of that scene to see here another "anointing" moment in David's career? Or are we perhaps meant to remember the danger that Samuel and the elders of Bethlehem saw in harboring an enemy of Saul? Perhaps both are in view.

David tells Ahimelech that he has been sent on a secret mission from Saul (1 Sam 23:2). Secrecy is obviously important to David's mission (for the sake of his survival) and he certainly comes from Saul (though, running from him). However, there can be no doubt that what David tells the priest must be conceived of as a lie. Which leads to the question of whether David's lie can be considered a moral act?

The results of David's deception will certainly be disastrous, as we will soon see. It is thus reasonable to characterize his actions here negatively. However, there is some significant narrative irony to David's dissembling that might characterize him a little differently.

After all, Saul has repeatedly sent David on missions where his intentions are secret (1 Sam 18:17 and 18:21–22), so perhaps we are meant to appreciate David's deception in using the concept of a secret mission as a cover up. Furthermore, David's deception here in keeping his true mission secret from Saul is very similar to Samuel's divinely approved deception in his mission to Bethlehem (1 Sam 16:2–5). Perhaps we might not judge David too harshly for lying to a priest. Although, I'm not sure we can ever escape the fact that the idea of lying to a priest just doesn't sound right.

In his interaction with Ahimelech, David procures some significant items. David asks for "bread, or whatever is here" (1 Sam 21:3 [4 MT]) and a "spear or sword" (1 Sam 21:8 [9 MT]). What David receives is the bread of the presence, which is especially dedicated for the priests, and the sword of Goliath. It is not hard for western readers to see some excalibur-like significance to this moment. While nothing much is made of the sword of Goliath after this, what is perhaps significant is what David asks for and what he receives. He requests two normal items. He receives two special or holy items. Perhaps this highlights the special treatment of David. But perhaps it also suggests a mixture of the sacred and the secular in David. Or, as Stephen Chapman suggests,

> The sword's religious significance is more important to the narrative than its military usefulness.... The point is rather that David continues to pursue a combination of strength *and* holiness, seeking strength *in* holiness, an impulse also found in Jonathan (1 Sam 14) but utterly lacking in Saul.[4]

David's actions at Nob lead to one of the darker moments in the David story. In between David's two requests the narrator informs us about a certain servant of Saul named Doeg the Edomite. This seemingly insignificant fact will have a big part to play soon.

David then flees to Achish, king of Gath, presumably with the sword of Goliath. The residents of Gath apparently remember David's reputation as a Philistine killer (1 Sam 21:11) and David coming to them with the sword of Goliath *of Gath*(!) probably does not help his case. Feigning madness, David escapes (1 Sam 21:12–15). Interestingly, David feigns madness, which leads to his escape from the Philistines, whereas Saul has suffered actual madness, which led to David's escape from him (1 Sam 18–19).

When the scene turns to a frustrated Saul complaining that no one tells him anything about what David is up to (1 Sam 22:7–8), a voice speaks up. It is a character whom the reader has just met, but one that was easy to ignore. It will be harder to ignore him now. Doeg speaks up and says, "I saw the son of Jesse[5] coming to Nob, to Ahimelech son of Ahitub; he inquired of the Lord for him, gave him provisions, and gave him the sword of Goliath the Philistine"

---

4. Chapman, *1 Samuel*, 176.

5. This is not the first time a servant of Saul has said "I have seen a son of Jesse" or some approximation of that. One of Saul's servants also claimed to have seen "a son of Jesse" when Saul is on the lookout for someone to play music for him in 1 Sam 16:18. The situation has changed somewhat since then.

(1 Sam 22:9–10). We note that the latter two of those claims is clear to the reader from the text, but the claim that Ahimelech inquired of the LORD for David is either a lie or is a gap in the narrative.[6]

Saul immediately sends for Ahimelech and all the priests of Nob. Saul's approach to this confrontation with Ahimelech is a series of accusing questions: "Why have you . . . ?" (1 Sam 22:13). Ahimelech claims innocence by defending what one assumes is the popular opinion of David: "Who among all your servants is so faithful as David?" (1 Sam 22:14). His rhetorical question to Saul, "Is today the first time that I have inquired of God for him?" (1 Sam 22:15), is ambiguous and could be taken as a confirmation that Ahimelech has indeed inquired of the LORD for David or as a denial of that fact.[7]

Saul response to Ahimelech is an order that Ahimelech and all the priests of the LORD from Nob be slaughtered (22:16–17). Just in case the reader was unsure whether or not the wholesale slaughter of priests of the LORD was a bad thing (it is!), we are told that Saul's own servants would "not raise their hand to attack the priests of the LORD" (1 Sam 22:17). Doeg, on the other hand, has no such compunction and proceeds to kill eighty-five priests (22:18). The slaughter does not end there, however. It grows beyond the priests and includes the entire city of Nob, "men and women, children and infants, oxen, donkeys, and sheep" (22:19). This is the language of *herem*, of holy war. What Saul refused to do to the Amalekites at God's command (1 Samuel 15), he carries out against his own people!

---

6. For discussion about whether or not to trust Doeg, see Bodner, *David Observed*, 32–33. Bodner suggests Doeg is probably not trustworthy in this instance.

7. For discussion, see Firth, *1 & 2 Samuel*, 240.

Run, David! Run!

What perhaps needs to be noted is that even in this abject horror and slaughter God's will is done and benefits David. That God's will is done in this horrific act can be seen in the fact that the first that are killed are the household of Ahimelech and those who wear the linen ephod. This is in fulfillment of the judgement oracle that the man of God brings on the house of Eli (1 Sam 2:27–36). Ahimelech as great-grandson of Eli (see 1 Sam 14:3) is on the receiving end of God's judgment on the house of Eli. That David benefits is seen in the fact that the slaughter causes Ahimelech's son Abiathar to flee to David (1 Sam 22:20). In the information warfare that will follow, the presence of Abiathar with David will feature prominently.

The last thing that remains of this horrible incident at Nob is David's response to it. Again, the narrative has one more surprise. David, it turns out, knew about Doeg's presence. He also had an idea of the ramifications that Doeg's presence would have (1 Sam 22:22), though perhaps he did not anticipate the extent and evil of Saul's reaction. Nevertheless, he takes some of the blame for the bloodshed at Nob. This last revelation provides an interesting characterization of David. He is characterized at least somewhat sympathetically. He takes Abiathar in. He takes part of the blame of the events at Nob. On the other hand, it is clear that David at least took a calculated risk by interacting with Ahimelech while Doeg was present. So, it is possible that David is presented as slightly calloused. As Barbara Green notes, perhaps David has "a tendency to use what others offer at their cost to his own gain."[8]

---

8. Green, *David's Capacity for Compassion*, 94.

It's Not What You Know, It's Who You Know (1 Samuel 23)

After the macabre events at Nob, David continues to be on the run. David learns that Philistines are fighting against Keilah, a fortified town of Judah (cf. Josh 15:44). It is not clear who told David this. The NRSV reads "Now they told David" (1 Sam 23:1), but this could just be a way of saying "it was told to David." Not knowing where this information comes from makes it feel a bit like coincidence. However, in the story-world of the Book of Samuel, coincidences always seem suspicious. It seems that often coincidence is evidence of providence.

David's response to this seemingly coincidental information is to inquire of the Lord (1 Sam 23:2). David will inquire of the Lord repeatedly in this chapter. It is significant and perhaps ironic for a number of reasons. First, the phrase "inquire of the Lord" is the very phrase that was used to describe Ahimelech's interaction with David in the previous episode (22:10, 13, 15). Second, the question of information is key. David regularly appears to rely on God for information, whereas Saul seems dependent on news from spies or other parties. Third, and perhaps ironically, the language of David "inquiring" of the Lord recalls Saul's name. The word "inquire" is the Hebrew word *sha'al*, which is the same root from which Saul's name, *Sha'ul*, comes. The theme of asking is a key one for Saul. The rationale that Hannah gives for naming her son Samuel, foreshadows Saul. She says, "I have asked (*sha'al*) him of the Lord" (1 Sam 1:20), clearly playing on Saul's name. Then the people "ask" (*sha'al*) for a king (1 Sam 8:10). So, although asking is thematically key for Saul (it is even the meaning of his own name), when it comes to asking of the Lord, David will have much more success. This is an important part of understanding these two characters. Finally, though we don't see it here, David's standard mechanism for asking of the LORD is regularly through the ephod that was brought to him by Ahimelech's son Abiathar (see 1 Sam 23:6).[9] Thus, in the information game, the means through which David most regularly successfully communicates with God is the very thing that came to him *because* of Saul's violent destruction at Nob. Saul is thus regularly thwarted because of his own past violent actions.

After saving Keilah, David learns that Saul was coming against him (again, we don't know how he knows). His response is to utilize the ephod to seek information from the LORD and confirm whether Saul really will come against him and whether the people of Keilah will surrender him to Saul (1 Sam 23:9–12). It turns out, they will. So much for gratitude. However, knowing that information turns out to be essential. Since, when David flees Keilah, Saul gives up pursuit (1 Sam 23:13).

Now in the wilderness of Ziph, David once again learns that Saul is seeking his life (1 Sam 23:15). This time, however, it is not information from God that brings him a solution and comfort, it is Saul's son Jonathan. Jonathan comes out to meet David in the wilderness and confirms to David his belief that David will be king over Israel and what's more, Saul knows this to be true (1 Sam 23:17). The best friends make another covenant, or perhaps renew their covenant, and Jonathan returns home. The royal encouragement is short lived, however, as the Ziphites inform Saul that David is hiding in their territory (1 Sam 23:19). Saul

---

9. The ephod was an item of priestly apparel that was apparently connected to the priestly breastpiece which contained the Urim and the Thummim, which were used for divining God's will. On the relation of the breastpiece and the ephod see Exod 28:4, 15, 26, and 28. On the location of the Urim and the Thummim within the priestly breastpiece see Exod 28:30 and Lev 8:8. On the Ephod generally see Meyers, "Ephod," 550.

thinks he has David yet again and asks the Ziphites to go spy out further where David is hiding. David learns that Saul is after him, once again, from an unnamed source, and flees to Maon. Saul continues his pursuit, but just as he is closing in on David (1 Sam 23:26), a messenger comes to him and tells him that the Philistines are attacking the land (1 Sam 23:27) so Saul must give up his pursuit and deal with those pesky Philistines. Another close call where David is lucky to elude Saul. Or perhaps he is not lucky. Perhaps his series of fortunate events shows what we have suggested before. In biblical narrative very often, coincidence is evidence of providence.

David, it seems, is able to escape Saul's grasp each time Saul gets close. Each time it is because he happens to learn about Saul's pursuit from an unnamed source or learns what Saul and others will do from the LORD through the Ephod, or happens to be saved by an unexpected Philistine attack that forces Saul to give up his pursuit of David. David seems one step ahead of Saul all this time. Saul keeps getting informed about David's whereabouts, but it doesn't seem enough. In this cat-and-mouse pursuit between Saul and David, perhaps it is less about *what* you know and more about *who* you know!

DAVID SPARES SAUL (1 SAMUEL 24–26)

David Spares Saul (1 Samuel 24, 26)

In chapter 24 we find the same scenario that we saw throughout chapter 23. Saul learns of David's whereabouts and pursues him. This time, however, he catches up to him and we actually get a confrontation. Saul takes 3,000 men and pursues David. Before finding him, however, he stops to relieve himself in a cave. To the enjoyment of those rooting for David, he just happens to pick the cave where David

Run, David! Run!

is hiding with his men. This must be some cave! With Saul alone and embarrassingly vulnerable, David's men encourage him to take advantage of the situation.

> The men of David said to him, "Here is the day of which the LORD said to you, 'I will give your enemy into your hand, and you shall do to him as it seems good to you.'"
>
> (1 Sam 24:4)

We, the reader, do not know about this promise from God since it is not recorded anywhere in the Book of Samuel. Is this a narrative gap that David's men are filling in for us? Or, are they making up a plausible promise that sounds like something God would have said? Either way, whether God made the promise or not, the issue is up to David to discern what seems good to him. It is worth pausing and reflecting on David's situation. For several chapters now, Saul has done nothing but try to kill him. God has promised David that he is the LORD's anointed. David's men seem to believe that God has told David that he will give David's enemy into his hand to do whatever is good to him, which is the kind of thing that God says to those he anoints (see 1 Sam 10:7).[10] It would thus be hard to blame David for believing that killing Saul and taking his place as the LORD's anointed is the right thing to do. That, however, is not what seems good to David. Apparently, what seems good to David is to cut off the corner of Saul's cloak (1 Sam 24:4), presumably as a warning.[11] This act of cutting of the corner of Saul's

---

10. V. Philips Long has made a strong case for Saul's failure to fulfill his charge to "do whatever you see fit to do" (1 Sam 10:7) as the key thing that signals Saul's unfitness for kingship. For a succinct presentation of his argument, see Long, *Art of Biblical History*, 201–23 or Long, "First and Second Samuel," 174–79.

11. This act is, of course, also rife with symbolic significance. David could be symbolizing cutting away the kingdom, just as a torn

cloak seems pretty tame considering his situation. David's response to this is thus somewhat surprising.

> Afterward David was stricken to the heart because he had cut off a corner of Saul's cloak. He said to his men, "The LORD forbid that I should do this thing to my lord, the LORD's anointed, to raise my hand against him; for he is the LORD's anointed."
>
> (1 Sam 24:5-6)

At least two things are worth noting about David's response to this action. First, David is said to be stricken to the heart. As we have noted, the theme of David's heart is significant and we will continue to see how this is so. For now, it is enough to note that we see an aspect of David's conscience. He feels regret for an action he had taken.

Second, his motivation for not striking Saul is his recognition that to strike the LORD's anointed would be an abominable thing. Now this could be interpreted as setting up a "no touching the LORD's anointed" policy, which will work significantly to David's benefit as one who is also the LORD's anointed.[12] However, given that this principle is introduced in the context of David's stricken heart, it is possible to see this as David being legitimately convicted about his actions. For all David's faults, and they are many, he is capable of recognizing his wrong action and capable of seeing it as a wrong act, even if it is not blatantly obvious why it is wrong, as here.

The exchange that follows between David and Saul does a number of things, but perhaps most importantly, we

---

robe signaled God taking the kingdom away from Saul and giving it to David (1 Sam 15:27-29). Cf. also the prophet Ahijah tearing up a robe to signal the dividing of the kingdom between Judah and Israel (1 Kgs 11:29-39).

12. See, for example, Alter, *The David Story*, 148.

see David's emphatic claim of innocence when it comes to his dealings with Saul and Saul's recognition that David is more righteous than he is because he has repaid Saul's evil with good (1 Sam 24:17). The chapter ends with this emphasis on David's innocence, Saul's understanding of David's innocence, and the surety that David will be the future king (1 Sam 24:21-22). David here is characterized by both restraint and regret. He restrains himself from killing Saul, but he also regrets the small action of symbolic violence that he does engage in.

Just two chapters later (ch. 26) one gets the sense of a glitch in the matrix as we read of another story in which the Ziphites again come and tell Saul where David is hiding and Saul again comes after David with 3,000 men. This time, however, instead of Saul fortuitously relieving himself alone in David's cave, David sneaks into Saul's camp at night with one of his warriors. Once again, David is in a position where Saul is vulnerable. This time he is asleep. Once again, David's men encourage him to view this coincidence as evidence of providence and suggest to David that God has given his enemy into his hand (1 Sam 26:8).[13]

David again refuses to raise his hand against the LORD's anointed (1 Sam 26:9-10). Once again, David takes something from Saul that shows his vulnerability to David and once again addresses Saul, though this time directly addressing Abner, accusing him of not protecting the king (1 Sam 26:14-16). And once again Saul recognizes he is wrong and promises not to seek David's life anymore (1 Sam 26:21, 25). The repetitiveness of this scene with the previous scene is easy to see. One thing that two repetitious scenes like this may do is communicate emphasis. Narrating two

---

13. This phrase recalls David's claim that God had given Goliath into his hand (1 Sam 17:46). It seems that David is not against interpreting advantageous situations as providence, just not this instance.

separate but very similar instances where David spares Saul affixes this aspect of David's character in our minds.

The repetitions between these stories are not exact, however. There are differences and some of them are significant. First, in the first story, David's action of cutting off the corner of Saul's robe led to David regretting that action and being stricken to the heart (1 Sam 24:5). In the second story, we get no sense of David's regret at taking the king's spear and water jar. Perhaps he has learned a lesson? Second, in the first story David decided not to strike down Saul because he would not raise his hand against the LORD's anointed. In the second story there is an additional piece of theological rationale. He understands that Saul's fate is in the LORD's hand, as he says, "As the LORD lives, the LORD will strike him down; or his day will come to die; or he will go down into battle and perish" (1 Sam 26:10). In other words, he understands that he is not to take Saul's fate into his own hands. Where did David learn this lesson? For that we need to turn to the chapter that is sandwiched by chapters 24 and 26.

David Confronts Saul Nabal (1 Samuel 25)

From chapter 19 through chapter 26 Saul has been relentlessly pursuing David. The shift in players in chapter 25 feels somewhat out of place. In the gaming world we would think of this chapter as a side quest. If this were a television series we would consider chapter 25 a character-driven episode that doesn't move the main plot forward much. However, as we will see, this chapter is very important for understanding David, especially as it is framed by these two scenes of David sparing Saul in ch. 24 and 26.

The new cast of characters in this scene are Abigail and Nabal, or the fair and the fool, respectively. Although they may be more complex characters than these labels may suggest,[14] they do nevertheless represent two poles of characterization. One of the questions that this story will ask is toward which pole does David lean?

The set-up is basically this: David hears that Nabal is shearing his sheep in Carmel and so sends men to the wealthy Nabal and states that he and his men have been protecting Nabal's shepherds in the wilderness and so asks that Nabal would "Please give whatever you have at hand" (1 Sam 25:8).[15] Nabal's response is not only to refuse David, but to insult him as well. "Who is David? Who is the son of Jesse?" Nabal dismissively asks (1 Sam 25:10). He accuses him of being a mere servant who has broken away from his master (1 Sam 25:10). This statement characterizes Nabal as a churl and also shows that Nabal actually knows exactly who David is.

David's reaction to these insults is rather intense: "Every man strap on his sword!" (1 Sam 25:13). There can be no confusing what he means by that response. David intends to take what he is owed by force. It is worth noting at this point that we, the reader, do not actually know who is in the right here. It could be that David is basically offering an invoice for services rendered in the wilderness. However, it could also be that David is operating a sort of protection racket and the only protecting that David is doing is protection from himself. The problem is that whatever happened in the wilderness happened off camera and we do not have access to that information. All we have are Nabal's and David's conflicting words. If David is offering an invoice, he is characterized one way, if he is running a protection racket,

14. On the potential complex portrayal of these characters, see Johnson, "Characters as Interpretive Crux," 5–8.

15. Interestingly, this sounds very much like David's request to Ahimelech (1 Sam 21:3).

he is characterized another way. This is what scholars call a "gap" in the narrative. It is a piece of information from the narrative that we do not have but need in order to understand fully what is going on.[16] We are forced to live in that gap at least for a little while. This means that we are left wondering about David, at least for a time.

The story continues and we have some confirmation of the situation. Hearing of Nabal's rude response to David, one of Nabal's own men run to Abigail and tell her 1) that Nabal is causing trouble, and 2) that David did in fact do what he said he did in the wilderness (1 Sam 25:14–15). The interesting thing about the young man's confirmation is that it only comes after the narrative has forced us to be at least a little suspicious about David's actions and intentions. David's name is cleared in this instance, but this is not the last time that this narrative will force us to question David's character and intentions.

After we gain some sympathies for David's perspective, the narrative continues with Abigail's actions. She springs to action and seeks to rectify her husband's insults by paying (or bribing?) David. Before Abigail meets David, the narrative then gives us a flashback to relive the moment when David responds to Nabal's insulting refusal. Not only did David tell everyone to strap on their sword, he swore a serious oath and promised that by morning there would be no one left to Nabal who "pisseth against the wall" (1 Sam 25:22 KJV). The issue is that this violent response seems to run counter to David's characterization in chapters 24 and 26, where David refused the violent course of action.[17] Even though Saul was seeking his life, David refused to kill him.

---

16. For a helpful discussion of "gaps" in biblical narrative, see Walsh, *Old Testament Narrative*, 65–80.

17. On the significance of the chapters 24 and 26 framing chapter 25 see Gordon, "David's Rise and Saul's Demise."

Nabal, on the other hand, merely insults him and that sends David into a murderous rage.

As David is on his way to murder Nabal and all the men of his household, Abigail meets him with gifts and pleads him to restrain himself from taking vengeance (1 Sam 25:26). This action, she says, would lead to "bloodguilt." David's intended actions, then, though somewhat understandable, given the fact that Nabal has wronged him, are in themselves wrong. How does this change our characterization of David? Jon Levenson has noted that where chapters 24 and 26 show David restraining himself, chapter 25 shows David's capacity for violence and darkness. "The episode of Nabal is the very first revelation of evil in David's character. He can kill. This time he stops short. But the cloud that chap. 25 raises continues to darken our perception of David's character."[18]

However, there is another element to David's characterization that comes up in this chapter. David takes admonishment from Abigail and changes his course of action. In chapter 24 he regretted his course of action. Now he allows another character to confront him and he changes his decisions accordingly. This interaction even picks up on the thematic thread of David's heart as Abigail tells him that killing Nabal and all his men would have caused "pangs of conscience" (1 Sam 25:31), or more literally, "a stumbling block of heart." In other words, David's heart, which has been judged "good" by God (1 Sam 16:7) and is said to be "after God's own heart" (1 Sam 13:14), would have stumbled if he had pursued his vengeance against Nabal. Some things, David learns, must be left in God's hands. And as the narrative progresses that is exactly what happens. *God* strikes Nabal and he dies (1 Sam 25:38). So when we hear David proclaim that David will not strike down Saul, but

18. Levenson, "1 Samuel 25," 23.

the LORD will strike him down; or his day will come to die; or he will go down into battle and perish" (1 Sam 26:10), this looks like a lesson he learned dealing with Saul's stand-in, Nabal.

CONCLUSION

We have now spent several chapters with David on the run. Perhaps these are not the most iconic chapters of David's life, but they do appear to be very significant. Like Forrest Gump, it appears that David learns some significant things while he is on the run from Saul.

First, in the cat-and-mouse game with Saul we learn that *what* you know is less significant than *who* you know. David's success in eluding Saul seems directly connected to the knowledge that he receives from God. Second, in his twofold encounter with Saul in the wilderness David has the opportunity to do Saul harm. In the first instance, at least he does something that he regrets. Apparently cutting off the corner of the king's robe is going too far in David's mind. Here we saw David be stricken to the heart. He develops his conviction that since Saul is still God's anointed, he is not to be touched. That David's heart is capable of regretting his actions is a significant thing to learn about David.

Finally, in his confrontation with Nabal, we learn that David has great capacity for violence and vengeance. Thankfully, we also learn that David is capable of taking course correction. In this case Abigail turns him aside and he avoids a "stumbling block of his heart." Here David takes a course correction and avoids the outcome of the worst aspects of his heart. Here we encounter both the dark side of David in his capacity for violence, but also capacity for change. It seems that there is much to learn from David on the run.

Run, David! Run!

EXCURSUS: ON SPELUNKING SPIRITUALITY[19]

Most scholarly readings of the character of David do not take the book of Psalms into account. The association between David and the Psalms is looser than popularly recognized by many Bible readers. The meaning of the superscription, "of David," is far from clear.[20] However, even within the narrative of Samuel, David has a reputation as a psalmist (see 2 Sam 1:17–27; 22:1–50; 23:1–7). Furthermore, whatever historical association between David and the Psalms we may discern, it is entirely hermeneutically legitimate to explore the relationship between David and the Psalms because of the superscriptions. So, what happens when we include the Psalms as providing some possible characterization of David? As an exploration of what happens when you allow the psalms to be included in our understanding of David's characterization, we will look at Psalm 142 and 1 Samuel 24.

The superscription of Psalm 142 reads "A Maskil of David. When he was in the cave. A Prayer." While there are a number of possible contexts when David is in a cave, a good case can be made for seeing the superscription as connecting this psalm with the cave at En-gedi in 1 Samuel 24. What happens when we read 1 Samuel 24 alongside Psalm 142? The results are interesting.

As we noted in the chapter above, the context of 1 Samuel 24 is David on the run from Saul. Throughout this section, the reader gets the clear sense that God is truly with David and God has clearly abandoned Saul, because David can do no wrong and Saul can do no right.

---

19. This excursus is adapted from Bodner and Johnson, "David: Kaleidoscope of a King," 133–36.

20. For various possible meanings, see Goldingay, *Psalms*, 24–26.

In that context we find David hiding in a cave when Saul comes in "to relieve himself" (1 Sam 24:3). David's men think that this is an opportunity given by God. David, however, just cuts off a corner of Saul's robe and then is "stricken to the heart" because of it (1 Sam 24:5).

When we look at Psalm 142 in light of this context, the results are a bit complex. On the one hand, Psalm 142 is a personal psalm, but a little generic. The voice of the psalm reflects that "they have hidden a trap for me" (Ps 142:3), "no refuge remains to me; no one cares for me" (Ps 142:4), "they [my persecutors] are too strong" (Ps 142:6). On the other hand, there are aspects of the psalm that do not seem to fit the context of David hiding in the cave in 1 Samuel 24. The psalmist speaks of numerous enemies leading a trap for him ("*they* have hidden a trap," v. 3), whereas David is on the run from Saul alone. The psalmist claims that "no one is concerned for me" (v. 4), whereas David has several hundred men with him. The psalmist laments to the LORD, "no one cares for my life" (v. 4), whereas the narrative has been clear in pointing out that Jonathan and Michal both clearly care for his life (chs. 19–20) and his men seem to care for his life by trying to convince him to dispatch his enemy. In many ways, the content of the psalm seems not to fit the context of the narrative. However, if, as creative interpreters, we read the scene of David in the cave of Eng-gedi with Psalm 142 offering some characterization of David, the results are fruitful and interesting.

In her discussion of Psalm 142, Vivian Johnson notes that if we read Psalm 142 as a prayer of David prior to Saul's arrival, then "when Saul enters the cave and David gains the upper-hand, it is not a coincidence. Rather, it is a divine act that comes about as an answer to David's prayer (Ps 142:4)."[21] This is a very interesting aspect of characterization

---

21. Johnson, *David in Distress*, 104.

because throughout the narrative of chapter 24 David's men have attributed this circumstance to God (1 Sam 24:4) and Saul has attributed it to God (1 Sam 24:19), but David does not explicitly attribute it to God. If we allow the psalm to characterize David, we are invited to see it as a response to David's prayer.

We can press this reading further. As we have noted, the whole narrative progression up to 1 Samuel 24 has made it clear that God is with David and God has abandoned Saul. Just as some movies and books put their heroes in danger but no one is actually concerned for the hero because we all know that they will be fine in the end, David's story can be read that way. David has no real reason to be afraid because we all know God is on his side. However, if we allow Psalm 142 to offer some of the character portrait for David, the picture becomes a little more nuanced than that.

Thus, while the David of the narrative may have no real reason to fear because we know God is with him, the David of the psalm can write of his spirit growing faint (Ps 142:3), of persecutors who are too strong for him (Ps 142:6). The David of the narrative has several hundred men surrounding him. The David of the psalm, however, can say that there is no one at his right hand, there is no one concerned for him, and that no one cares for his life (Ps 142:4). As far as David is concerned, he is in that cave alone. As a piece of dramatic characterization, it depicts David as someone who is surrounded by people and yet feels utterly alone. This is an interestingly relevant piece of characterization for our contemporary culture, which is more connected to others than ever before and yet reports of depression and loneliness are extremely high. Thus, when 1 Samuel 24 is read in light of Psalm 142, not only is the theological aspect of God's delivery of David heightened, but the dramatic and personal agony of David is given much greater emphasis.

QUESTIONS FOR REFLECTION

1. How would you describe David's journey as a character in these chapters? Does he grow in any discernible way?
2. We noted that the episode with Nabal showed that David has a "dark side." What do you make of that revelation in your understanding of David?
3. Psalms 52, 54, and 57 all have superscriptions which point to this section of David's life. Try reading one or more of these psalms alongside these narratives. What happens to your reading of the psalm when you do so? What happens to your reading of the narrative?

5

WHOSE SIDE ARE YOU ON?
1 Samuel 27–31

> "Is this not David, of whom they sing to one another in dances, 'Saul has killed his thousands, and David his ten thousands'?"
>
> —Philistine lords[1]

> "I know that you are as blameless in my sight as an angel of God."
>
> —Achish, king of Gath[2]

IN MY VIEW, ONE of the most surprisingly enjoyable and entertaining movies of the early 2000s was *Pirates of the Caribbean*, the first one, not the second, or third, or however many subpar sequels now exist. The first one is a classic, probably because no one expected a movie based on

1. 1 Sam 29:5.
2. 1 Sam 29:8.

a Disneyland ride to be any good. But we were all blown away by Johnny Depp's Captain Jack Sparrow. Is there a better and more fitting entrance of any character in film than Jack Sparrow's entrance, standing grandly on the mast of a sinking dinghy? The reason Jack Sparrow comes to mind as we turn to look at David's sojourn amongst the Philistines, is his penchant for playing both sides. At one point, during the climactic fight scene, Elizabeth, seeing Jack Sparrow fighting against the villainous Captain Barbosa, says to Will, "Whose side is Jack on?" To which Will replies, "At the moment..." and gives a little shrug. And of course, that is the point. Jack Sparrow is clearly on his own side and how he relates to other "sides" is a little difficult to pin down. Similarly, in this stretch of text, David's side is a little hard to pin down. He was one of Saul's captains, he is a famous slayer of Philistines, but he finds himself a Philistine mercenary faced with the possibility of fighting *with* the Philistines *against* Saul and Israel. It is an appropriate question for this stretch of the narrative to ask, "Whose side is David on?" and the answer is, "At the moment...."

FLEEING TO THE PHILISTINES (1 SAMUEL 27)

> David said in his heart, "I shall now perish one day by the hand of Saul; there is nothing better for me than to escape to the land of the Philistines; then Saul will despair of seeking me any longer within the borders of Israel, and I shall escape out of his hand."
>
> (1 Sam 27:1)

This portion of the narrative begins with David's internal monologue. Although saying something in your heart is a standard way to narrate internal monologue in Old

Testament narrative,[3] the reference to David's heart clues us in to a theme that we have been tracing. So, while it may be that this is simply the standard way to say this, it may be that this reference to David's heart clues us in to the fact that this is a key "heart" moment for David.

What David says in his heart is that he fears that Saul will eventually get him. On the one hand, this is completely understandable. Saul has been trying to kill him for eight chapters now. David is tired of running for his life. On the other hand, one of the lessons that David is supposed to have been learning is the importance of dependence upon God. This was the lesson that all Israel was supposed to learn in David's victory over Goliath (1 Sam 17:46–47). It was the lesson that we have been drawing from David's dependence upon inquiring of the LORD throughout the previous chapters (esp. ch. 23). And it is the lesson that we assume David learned in his dealings with Nabal (1 Sam 25). So are we perhaps meant to interpret what is happening in David's heart as a crisis of faith?[4] Perhaps that is too strong and Paul Evans' view that "David was human, and in a moment of doubt he made what seemed like the best decision he could at the time"[5] is on the right track.

At the very least, then, the narrative that follows is not the result of David's faith. It is the result of his struggle to know where to trust God to act and where to trust his own actions. This complex reality is something that all people of faith face and one that feels true to life.

So, David flees to Achish, who is king of Gath. This may seem a little surprising since David rose to prominence by killing the champion of Gath, Goliath! His plan seems

---

3. For example, Gen 8:21; 27:41; Deut 8:17; 1 Kgs 12:26; Hos 7:2; Eccl 2:15; Esth 6:6. See Ska, *"Our Fathers Have Told Us,"* 67–68.

4. So Edelman, *King Saul*, 232–33.

5. P. Evans, *Samuel*, 273. Cf. also Firth, *Samuel*, 284.

to have worked, since once Saul learns that David has fled to Gath he doesn't chase after him anymore (1 Sam 27:4). Nevertheless, as David rises in influence as a Philistine vassal, his activity begins to become somewhat suspect. Once Achish has trusted him enough to put him in charge of his own city, Ziklag, we begin to learn about David's raiding activity.

David goes out and attacks the Geshurites, the Girzites, and the Amalekites. These groups appear to be groups of people that Israel was supposed to have devoted to destruction, which perhaps alleviates some of the angst at David's slaughter.[6] However, it is hard to sanction David's actions here. First, not only does he raid these people, but we are told twice that he leaves neither man nor woman alive (1 Sam 27:9, 11) as if to emphasize the slaughter. Second, the reason for David's total slaughter is not obedience to the command of total destruction (from Deut 7:20), but so that word won't get out about whom David is attacking (1 Sam 27:11). After all, David is telling Achish that he is attacking Judahites (1 Sam 27:10), making Achish think that he is truly loyal to him and no longer loyal to Israel. Finally, we are told that this is his practice throughout the time that he dwelt amongst the Philistines (1 Sam 27:11), suggesting that the only reason for the slaughter was to cover up David's activity to Achish.

The lessons of the previous chapters suggest that David's activity here should be viewed in a negative light. One of the key differences between Saul and David in the previous chapters was David's repeated inquiring of the LORD. We will see David return to that practice, but there is no mention of David inquiring of the LORD here in his decision

---

6. The Geshurites are mentioned in Josh 13:1–2 and the Amalekites were supposed to be destroyed by Saul (1 Sam 15). See Firth, *Samuel*, 285–86; and Bergen, *Samuel*, 261–62.

to utterly wipe out the settlements of these people of the land. Additionally, as we noted above, David's dependence upon God has been a lesson that we, the readers, and David should have been learning throughout this story. Reflecting on this, Stephen Chapman argues the following:

> if the logic of bloodshed that David has articulated and adopted is true, then there cannot ever be a possibility of offensive warfare for Israel except at the express bidding of God (e.g., 1 Sam 15:2–3?). David's raids result from no divine mandate and therefore become a negative example in the text, an implicit question for consideration. And the narrative is finally willing to show David in an unsavory light if it will prod the reader into such further reflection.[7]

We are thus left reflecting on the fact that David's questionable decision to flee to the Philistines has forced him to another questionable course of action. The grey areas of David's sojourn amongst the Philistines do not end here.

After reading about David's vicious and questionable raiding practices, we are confronted with the main conflict of this portion of the story. The Philistines gather to fight against Israel, as they are apparently wont to do. Achish comes to David and says, "You know, of course, that you and your men are to go out with me in the army" (1 Sam 28:1). And there it is. David has been shedding copious amounts of blood to cover up the fact that he is not willing to attack Israelites. Now, however, Achish is coming to inform him that he is going to go out and face Israel in battle and David is required to come along. In the 1990s there was a popular Christian bracelet that had the letters WWJD on them. The idea was Christians ought to live their lives asking the question What Would Jesus Do (WWJD)? Well,

---

7. Chapman, *1 Samuel*, 199.

now we are faced with the very serious issue of WWDD: What Would *David* Do?

The response David gives to Achish's ultimatum that he will be fighting for the Philistines against the Israelites is to say, "Very well, then you shall know what your servant can do" (1 Sam 28:2). As far as cryptic responses go, this one is fantastic. Just exactly what does David mean here? Is this a confirmation that Achish can count on David? Or, is this an ambiguous statement that suggests to the reader who is paying attention that if it comes to it, Achish will know what David can do because he will find himself facing David in battle? Or, is this meant to reflect that David himself is conflicted about what he would do if forced to face Saul and Israel in battle? We may have our suspicions as to which it is, but the narrative leaves us hanging by changing the scene to tell us about Saul's attempt to inquire of the dead prophet, Samuel. Perhaps Netflix has spoiled us to cliffhangers, but as Walter Brueggemann has noted, the "break in the narrative after 28.2 is like watching a Saturday afternoon film serial, and needing to wait a week to see what will happen to the endangered hero."[8] Perhaps we ought to thank Disney+ and their practice of releasing one episode a week for the reminder of the narrative importance of building tension over time.

FIGHTING FOR THE PHILISTINES? (1 SAMUEL 29)

1 Samuel 28 narrates Saul's famous meeting with the medium of Endor and the consultation with the shade of Samuel. One of the functions of this episode is to foreshadow and build the tension for the confrontation that is about to happen as Samuel tells Saul that he and his sons will join Samuel in death tomorrow and God will give Israel into the

8. Brueggemann, *David and His Theologian*, 127.

hands of the Philistines (1 Sam 28:16–19). For the reader, the coming conflict has become all the more ominous. We know the outcome related to Saul and the Philistines, but we still don't know where David will be. David's dilemma, however, is solved for him. He never has to make the choice.

As chapter 29 opens, the Philistines are gathering for war and David and his men are present with Achish. In Texas, where I live, we "remember the Alamo." In Philistia, apparently, they "remember Goliath." The lords of the Philistines ask, "What are these Hebrews doing here?" (1 Sam 29:3). They ask, "Is this not David, of whom they sing to one another in dances, 'Saul has killed his thousands, and David his ten thousands'?" (1 Sam 29:5), which is, of course, the song that the women sang when David defeated Goliath (1 Sam 18:7). We know that the Philistines have some justification for their opinion of David. He has, after all, made his name as a slayer of Philistines. Achish, however, has a very different opinion of David. Three times in this chapter he stresses David's innocence (1 Sam 29:3, 6, 9–10).

Walter Brueggemann has argued that this threefold statement of David's innocence "is the central interest of the narrative."[9] However, the emphasis on David's innocence is complicated here. For one, it seems that Achish has a much too lofty view of David. David is many things but "blameless . . . as an angel of God" (1 Sam 29:9) is not one of them! For another, the narrative may just be leading us to doubt whether or not Achish has judged David rightly. So while the narrative causes us to dwell on statements about David's innocence, it also causes us to question any simple assessment about him.

Brueggemann, however, is right to see that this statement from Achish does reinforce something true to the characterization of David. For Achish says that David is

9. Brueggemann, *David and His Theologian*, 129.

"blameless," which is a rendering of the Hebrew word more simply translated "good" (*tov*). When Samuel tells Saul that God is replacing him with his neighbor in chapter 15, he tells Saul that God is appointing someone who is "better" (*tov*) than Saul (1 Sam 15:28). More recently, we have seen Saul claim that David is more righteous than he is for doing "good" (*tov*) toward him in spite of the evil that Saul has done toward David (1 Sam 24:17, 19; cf. 26:23). So while David is far from perfect and he may or may not be trustworthy the way Achish thinks he is, Achish's testimony about David does cause us to recall some *good* things about David.

We still do not know, however, David's loyalty. When Achish informs David that he not be part of the battle, David responds, "But what have I done? What have you found in your servant from the day I entered your service until now, that I should not go and fight against the enemies of my lord the king?" (1 Sam 29:8). Why would David object at all? If, as we assume, one of the dilemmas of David's sojourn amongst the Philistines was how to stay loyal to Israel while serving the Philistines, then David has been given an easy out. Why object? Is it purely to make a show of loyalty when he knows it won't be an issue? Or is this just a moment to torture readers with the confusion about where David's loyalties really lie? One of the issues with this statement is the ambiguity of it. Who exactly does David mean when he says he would "fight against the enemies of my lord the king?" Which king is he referring to here? Achish? Saul? This is that torturous ambiguity of this portion of the narrative.

Yael Shemesh has made a strong case that David is relentlessly loyal throughout his service to king Achish, but the ambiguity is meant to be enjoyed by the reader, who can see in David's ambiguous language his duping of king

Achish. One of the provocative points that she makes is that on her reading both Achish and Saul have mirrored misconceptions about David:

> both monarchs were totally mistaken in their evaluation of David's loyalty. But their misconceptions were mirror images of each other: Saul viewed David as his bitter enemy, when in fact David was loyal to him; Achish thought David was his faithful vassal, when in fact David deceived him, remained loyal to Saul and Israel, and posed a serious threat to Achish.[10]

Shemesh's argument is strong and the text is probably pushing the reader in that direction. However, the troubling fact is that we can never be fully sure of just what David would have done if he had been forced to face Saul in battle.[11] David is saved, not by his own decision, but by chance. Perhaps, we ought to see God saving David from having to make this decision. If we read the story this way we might see God being faithful to David even when David was not quite fully trusting in God. Or, perhaps, we see God living in light of the principle that the apostle Paul will later articulate, God "will not let you be tested beyond your strength" (1 Cor 10:13). Did God know that this particular test would be too hard for David to pass?

OUT OF THE PHILISTINE FRYING PAN (1 SAMUEL 30)

It seems to be a principle of the Star Wars movies that each main character needs some important mission to complete at the finale. In the *Return of the Jedi*, for example, Han and

10. Shemesh, "David in the Service of King Achish of Gath," 89.

11. On the undecidability of David's loyalty here, see Miscall, *1 Samuel*, 175.

Leia must disable the force field on Endor, Lando must lead the assault on the Death Star, and Luke must face the Emperor. Never mind the fact that the successful assault on the Death Star leaves Luke's confrontation somewhat redundant. Narratively, Luke needed to confront the emperor.

This section of David's story has been leading us toward this climactic conflict between Saul and the Philistines. However, David has just been removed from the conflict, leaving him with nothing to do for this climactic portion of the story. That's not right. The hero needs something to do. Let him fight the emperor! I mean, bring on the Amalekites! Instead of avoiding conflict by not being present with Achish, David jumps from the Philistine frying pan into the Amalekite fire.

Returning home to Ziklag, David learns that the Amalekites have raided his town and taken everyone captive (1 Sam 30:1–2). The scope of this tragedy for David and his men is evident as David's tough fighting force are said to weep "until they had no more strength to weep" (1 Sam 30:4). Given their own raiding practices (leaving no one alive), they have a right to weep. Things get even worse for David. His own men begin to think of stoning him (1 Sam 30:6). Perhaps they have a right. They have been following David and now their families are gone. David has gone from facing the choice of siding with the Philistines against Saul and the Israelites to the reality of his own loyal Israelites turning on him. What David does is somewhat surprising.

For the first time since David has entered Philistine service, he turns to the LORD. He "strengthened himself in the LORD his God" (1 Sam 30:6) and he consults the LORD through the Ephod for the first time since chapter 23. It seems that there is an important turning point here.[12] Faced with what appears the biggest tragedy of his career thus far

12. Cf. Firth, *Samuel*, 305–6.

and one that has the most obvious course of action, David turns to God.

He receives a positive response from God that he should pursue, and he does. However, 200 of his men were too exhausted to continue pursuit, and he leaves them behind. This seemingly insignificant fact will play a role shortly. In their pursuit, they just happen to come across an Egyptian slave to an Amalekite who had been left behind because he fell ill (1 Sam 30:13). This Egyptian then leads David and his men to the raiding party. David attacks them. About 400 Amalekites escape, suggesting that the size of the Amalekite raiding party was much bigger than David's 400 men. So, David recovers all that was taken. Nothing was missing and, we assume, no one was missing. David then comes to the 200 who were too exhausted to continue and offers them their share of the spoil. Some "worthless fellows" amongst David's men object to this, stating that since they did not fight, they should not receive any spoils (1 Sam 30:22). David, however, states that all will share equally. The reason he appears to give is that the spoil was "what the LORD has given us" (1 Sam 30:23). David now attributes his victory to God. After several chapters where God does not feature, David has suddenly turned toward God with some regularity. This practice becomes a principle for how Israel will operate from now on (1 Sam 30:25).

CONCLUSION

We began this chapter with the reflection that David appeared to be operating from a heartfelt position of doubt. Saul's pursuit had him doubting that God would protect him and so he took measures to protect himself. After that decision David enacted the questionable practice of mass murder to protect himself. The fact that he was raiding non-Israelite towns that were supposed to be devoted to destruction in the first place seems only to alleviate the horror of this action partially. He is then faced with the choice whether he would be willing to face Saul and the Israelites in battle. Although the narrative seems to lead us to the suggestion that David would have stayed loyal to Israel, we are kept from knowing that for certain and David is perhaps kept from having to face that decision. Finally, however, at the lowest moment in David's Philistine sojourn he turns toward God and rescues his people, giving God credit for the victory.

Like the infamous captain Jack Sparrow, we noted that the question that this chapter was getting us to ask was just where David's loyalties lie. He was going to have to wrestle with that decision and so were we. However, the journey that he goes on during this section of the narrative is one from some level of doubt to seemingly reaffirming his faith and dependence upon God. Perhaps then, the answer to the question about loyalties that David and we, the readers, are supposed to come to is a reaffirmed loyalty towards God.

QUESTIONS FOR REFLECTION

1. Consider David's practice of total destruction in his raids in 1 Samuel 27:8–12. Are you comfortable with this practice? How do you think this characterizes David?
2. Do you think David would have been faithful to Achish if he had been forced to be present at the battle against Israel? Why or why not?
3. Throughout this portion of his story David seems to journey from doubt to questionable decisions to ultimately turning back to God at his darkest moment. In what ways do you resonate with this journey?

ƒ

CONSOLIDATION AND COVENANT

2 Samuel 1–9

> "How the mighty have fallen in the midst of battle! Jonathan lies slain upon your high places. I am distressed for you, my brother Jonathan."
>
> "I will make myself yet more contemptible than this."
>
> "Who am I, O Lord God, and what is my house, that you have brought me thus far?"
>
> —David[1]

IN THE HIT BROADWAY musical, *Hamilton,* about the life of treasury secretary Alexander Hamilton, the climactic moment of victory in the revolutionary war only marks the midway point of the play. The second half of the show is

---

1. 2 Sam 1:25–26; 6:22; 7:18.

about the drama and dueling, the battles and betrayals that happened after America won its independence. Similarly, in David's story, although the bulk of the narrative has led us to the moment when David will be king in Israel, as was promised, the moment when Saul is killed and the way is paved for David to be king marks only the halfway point. The rest of the story will be the drama and dueling, the battles and betrayals that happened after Saul is dead and the way is opened for David to be made king in Israel.

CONSOLIDATION (2 SAMUEL 1–6)

David's Lament (2 Samuel 1)

The first several chapters of 2 Samuel deal with the events that happen in the immediate aftermath of Saul's death. In chapter 1, the death of Saul is narrated again, this time from the perspective of the Amalekite who claims to have been the one who killed the injured Saul (2 Sam 1:10).[2] David's response to the Amalekite's claim to have dispatched the king of Israel is quite drastic, but it is in keeping with his "hands off of the LORD's anointed" policy. He has the Amalekite killed on the spot on the basis of his own testimony of killing Saul (2 Sam 1:15–16).

David's response to the news of the death of Saul and Jonathan is one of mourning. After mourning and fasting until evening (2 Sam 1:12) and having Saul's killer executed, David offers a formal lamentation for Saul and Jonathan. Although we cannot fully do this poem justice in such a

---

2. There are discrepancies between the death of Saul as narrated in 1 Samuel 31 and the death of Saul as reported by the Amalekite in 2 Samuel 1. The differences can probably be attributed to some storytelling license on the part of the Amalekite. For a good discussion, see Bergen, *Samuel*, 287–88.

Consolidation and Covenant

brief treatment, there are a number of aspects of this poem that help us further understand David.

First, we need to understand the significance of this poem in the Book of Samuel. Many have noticed that the Book of Samuel is framed by four significant poems. At the start there is Hannah's song (1 Sam 2:1–10). At the center is David's lament for Saul and Jonathan (2 Sam 1:17–27). At the end are David's two poems (2 Sam 22:1–51 and 23:1–7). These poems thematically frame the book. Hannah's song is kingship *anticipated*, David's lament for Saul and Jonathan is the failure of kingship *lamented*, and the final two poems are reflections God's kingship *celebrated*.[3] So David's lament is at the heart of the Book of Samuel and occurs at the turning point where we move from the reign of Saul to the reign of David.

We must recognize the broader theological and literary significance of this poem. However, we will do it injustice if we do not also recognize its significance as a poem of personal lament on the part of David. It must be noted that there is potential for ambiguity in the poem. As others have argued, while it is intensely personal, it is also good PR for David and thus its motivations are always possibly suspect.[4]

The bulk of the poem includes moving imagery of tragedy. He laments the fall of Saul and Jonathan, whom he refers to as "mighty ones" (2 Sam 1:19, 25, 27). He exhorts that news of the death of the royal father and son should not be told in Philistine cities, so that their enemies would not exult in their deaths (2 Sam 1:20). The poem celebrates Saul and Jonathan even while it mourns their death. The climax of the poem comes at the end when it turns very personal and is clearly David's lament for Jonathan rather

---

3. Cf. Firth, *Samuel*, 321.

4. For one recent attempt to get at the complexity of this poem, see Linafelt, "Private Poetry and Public Eloquence."

than a generic lament for the leaders of Israel. Saul fades to the background and Jonathan comes into focus.

> "How the mighty have fallen
> in the midst of the battle!
>
> Jonathan lies slain upon your high places.
> I am distressed for you, my brother Jonathan;
> greatly beloved were you to me;
> your love to me was wonderful,
> passing the love of women.
>
> How the mighty have fallen,
> and the weapons of war perished!"
>
> (2 Sam 1:25–27)

This last part of the poem marks intense and personal language. The significance of this is that David has not been a character to wear any of his heart on his sleeve. In fact, we have noted that we frequently do not know what David thinks or how David feels. Very rarely do we see insight into David's character. Here, however, I think we see David's personal commitment to and affection for his friend Jonathan. As we noted in the excursus to chapter 3 on the David-and-Jonathan relationship, this is a place where commentators have regularly seen homoerotic overtones to David and Jonathan's relationship. As I stated above, I find this unlikely and not evident in the text. The language of this poem certainly portrays intimate relationship and feelings, but it suggests much more clearly the intimate feelings of an ancient warrior's bond rather than any idea of a homosexual relationship.[5] So, although the death of Saul and Jonathan are politically significant for David, his lament suggests that they are personally significant for him

---

5. Cf. the comments of Alter, *The David Story*, 200–201 and the excursus in chapter 3 above.

as well, perhaps primarily so. He does not vilify the house of Saul but celebrates them. He does not rejoice that the way to the throne is open. He laments it.

Civil War (2 Samuel 2–5)

Although Saul is dead, that is not the end of the Saulide line. David's path to the throne is clearer than it was before Saul died, but it is not entirely clear. There is an entire game of thrones that needs to be played out before David can be crowned king of Israel.

Following the news of the death of Saul and Jonathan and David's lament, we read of the crowning of the two rival kings: David (2 Sam 2:1–7) and Ishbaal (2 Sam 2:8–11). Here David again inquires of the LORD before he goes up and chooses a place for his base of operations (2 Sam 2:1). So David is still in the mode of regularly seeking God's guidance. Furthermore, after being anointed as king of Judah, David learns that the people of Jabesh-gilead buried Saul after his death at Philistine hands, and David blesses them (2 Sam 2:5–7).

The existence of two rival kings, of course, leads to conflict and the rest of chapter 2 narrates some of the violent clashes that happen between the house of Saul and the house of David. Much of this clash will be between Saul's general, Abner,[6] and David's general and nephew, Joab. Abner, Saul's general, has been known to us since David has come on the scene in 1 Samuel 17. Joab, on the other hand, is only now coming to prominence in the narrative. Perhaps the most significant moment in these clashes is the death of Asahel, the younger brother of Joab, at the hand of Abner (2 Sam 2:18–23). This sets up animosity between Abner and Joab.

6. Presumably the real power in the house of Saul (cf. 2 Sam 2:9).

After the narration of the first hostilities between Israel and Judah, we hear of trouble in the house of Saul as Ishbaal accuses Abner of taking Saul's concubine, Rizpah, for himself (2 Sam 3:7). The narrative does not confirm one way or another whether this is true or not. Abner denies it vehemently. However, his defense feels a bit like it breaks the Hamlet principle. He "doth protest too much."[7] Consequently, Abner contacts David, telling him that he will defect to David (2 Sam 3:12). David accepts Abner's deal with the provision that he wants Abner to return his first wife, Michal, to him (2 Sam 3:13–14). Remember, that Michal, who had helped save him from Saul (1 Samuel 19), was given to Paltiel (1 Sam 25:44). Perhaps, romantically, we might think that this is the conclusion of a tragic love story and David will be reunited with his first love. However, the way that the relationship between David and Michal unfolds from here on out suggests that it is more likely that David is playing politics and having his Saulide bride returned to him in order to strengthen his right to the throne of Israel.[8] Michal is returned while her husband, Paltiel, follows behind her weeping. While the text does not explicitly say that Paltiel loved Michal, the picture of the weeping husband following his wife as more powerful men take her away does leave the impression that Michal is leaving a personal relationship for a political one.

David gets the better of this deal than Abner. After David has solidified his deal with Abner and Abner goes off to rally Israel for David, Joab learns of David's peace agreement. Joab states his suspicions of Abner (2 Sam 3:24–25), but the reader also recalls that Abner is the killer of Joab's

---

7. *Hamlet*, Act III, Scene II. Cf. Bodner, *David Observed*, 48.

8. On the role of women, generally, in the David story and Michal specifically, see Westbrook, "And He Will Take Your Daughters," 45–63, 87–109.

little brother Asahel (2 Sam 2:22–23). Joab follows after Abner and kills him "for shedding the blood of Asahel" (2 Sam 3:27). David's response to learning of Abner's death is to declare his innocence and to condemn and curse Joab for the killing (2 Sam 3:28–29). David then intones a lament for Abner (2 Sam 3:33–34), which is more brief than his lament for Saul and Jonathan. However, it is significant that David seems constantly to be officially mourning the death of his enemies. The result, according to the narrator, is that the people "understood that day that the king had no part in the killing of Abner son of Ner" (2 Sam 3:37). The result, according to many readers, is that now *David* appears to be protesting too much himself and our suspicions have risen.[9]

This portion of the narrative closes off with the scene of the brothers Rechab and Baanah, who kill Saul's son, Ishbaal, in his sleep (2 Sam 4:4–7). Thinking they will gain a reward, they take his head to David (2 Sam 4:8). Like the Amalekite who had claimed to kill Saul, David has them killed (2 Sam 4:12). And although he does not claim that Ishbaal is the LORD's anointed, as Saul was, murdering an innocent man is punished with swift and permanent justice. The reader is forgiven for thinking there may be a slight inconsistency in David's justice here, as he accused Joab of doing this very thing and he appears to have not received the same kind of justice as Rechab and Baanah.

In the aftermath of this civil war, the elders of Israel come to David and make him king of all Israel (2 Sam 5:1–5). He eventually takes Jerusalem from the Jebusites and makes it his own city (2 Sam 5:6–10). "And David became greater and greater, for the LORD, the God of hosts was with him" (2 Sam 5:10). The whole narrative seems to be coming to a conclusion, as David is now on the throne and

---

9. On a suspicious reading of David's actions here, see VanderKam, "Davidic Complicity"; and Bodner, *David Observed*, 38–66.

his rule is being consolidated from the house of Saul and will shortly be consolidated from other external enemies (2 Sam 5:17–25).

COVENANT (2 SAMUEL 6–9)

Returners of the Lost Ark (2 Samuel 6)

Before it was found by Indiana Jones, the ark of the covenant plays an interesting role in David's story. In 2 Samuel 7 we will get to perhaps the most significant moment in the life of David: God's promise to David and his household. However, before we get there, we must briefly discuss the story of the returners of the lost ark.

Having been made king of Israel and Judah in the previous chapter, David now goes out to retrieve the ark from Baale-judah,[10] where it had remained since it was returned from the Philistines in 1 Samuel 6–7. David, it seems, is now setting up Jerusalem as the spiritual center of Israel as well as the political power center. Things do not go smoothly, however, as Uzzah, son of Abinadab, who had housed the Ark, is struck down by God for reaching out his hand to the ark when it shook on the ox cart (2 Sam 6:6–7). A number of things are significant about this event. First, the description of the ark being driven on a "new cart" is more reminiscent of the way the Philistines transported the ark (1 Sam 6:7) than the way that the Pentateuch prescribes carrying the ark (see Exod 25:13–15; cf. Num 4:1–18). Second, if the way the LORD struck the men of Beth-shemesh (1 Sam 6:19) was to show Israel that God could strike Israelites down for inappropriate attitude toward God and his presence, just as he did with the Philistines, then that lesson

---

10. This is probably to be equated with Kiriath-jearim, which is where the ark was last referenced in 1 Samuel 7.

still stands. David needs to learn that the ark and the presence of God that it represented was not under his control.[11] The seemingly minor infraction of touching the ark, was more serious than David, or certainly Uzzah, understood.

David's desire to move the ark to Jerusalem is only delayed, however, as he eventually brings the ark to Jerusalem with much celebration, shouting, and, in David's case, dancing (2 Sam 6:12–15). Although the moment is celebratory, not everyone feels like partying. Looking out over the procession from her window, Michal, who once loved David, now looks with scorn at David dancing before the ark (see 2 Sam 6:20). David's response "I have danced before the LORD. I will make myself yet more contemptible than this" (2 Sam 6:21–22) does not show a happy household. As someone whose story started with her love for David and her willingness to defy her father to save him, we can probably forgive Michal her bitterness. Since those early chapters she has been nothing more than a political pawn. One thing that it certainly shows is that even though David proclaimed innocence in relation to Saul's death, lives were ruined in his maneuvering for the throne.[12]

Covenant (2 Samuel 7)

We come now to perhaps the most significant moment in David's life and one of the most significant chapters in the whole Old Testament. Superfluous statements about the significance of 2 Samuel 7 abound. One commentator suggests that it contains, "the most crucial theological statement in the Old Testament."[13]

11. Cf. Firth, *Samuel*, 376.

12. For more on Michal's story, see Westbrook, *"And He Will Take Your Daughters,"* 97–109.

13. Brueggemann, *Samuel*, 259.

The story opens with David's desire to build a house for God (2 Sam 7:1). David is not without biblical rationale for this desire. According to Deuteronomy, when God grants Israel peace from all their enemies, they will bring everything into the place that "God will choose as a dwelling for his name" (Deut 12:10–11). We know that David has peace from his enemies (2 Sam 7:1). So David's inquiry to the prophet Nathan about a "house" for the LORD seems justifiable.

David observes to the prophet Nathan that he lives in a royal house of cedar while God lives in a mere tent (2 Sam 7:2), suggesting that David should do something about this. Nathan approves of David's idea, stating "Go, do all that you have in mind; for the LORD is with you" (2 Sam 7:3). What the NRSV has translated as "mind" is actually the word "heart." So, Nathan has told David, "Go, do all that you have in your *heart*." Nathan is also not without justification for his views. We have stated throughout this study that God appears to be approving of David's heart (1 Sam 13:14; 16:7). And the story has been clear that God is with David in a special way (e.g., 1 Sam 16:18; 18:12, 14, 28; 2 Sam 5:10). All signs point to David building a house for God sounding like a good idea. However, sounding like a good idea is not the same as being a good idea.

God's response to this proposal is to ask a simple question: Did I ask for this? (2 Sam 7:4–7). God does not outright refuse David, but merely asks a question that implies the answer: no. We have seen a number of factors that lead us to assume that Nathan was right to think that David's idea was a good one. But the important factor seems to be that it wasn't God's idea, so its merits do not matter.

The question is, however, why would God refuse to let David build a house for him? One answer is given in later texts. It is suggested that David, as a man of violence,

Consolidation and Covenant

is unfit to build a house for God (see 1 Kgs 5:3; 1 Chr 22:8; 28:3). A second answer may be suggested by God's own rhetoric. "Shall *you* build for *me* a house for *my* name?"[14] The importance may be that the decision to build a house for God cannot be a human initiative. As the text from Deuteronomy 12 stated, the place for God's name will be the place that *"God* will choose" (Deut 12:10). Another related answer is the importance for God to establish the appropriate relationship between God and David. It is possible that David's decision to move the ark to Jerusalem was an attempt to force God into his sphere of power. He had to learn a lesson at the cost of the life of Uzzah. David needs to learn that there is nothing he can do to bind God to himself. As Walter Brueggemann helpfully states,

> Too much had been taken for granted in the happy link between king and God. Now it is time for high theology, for [God] here disassociates himself from conventional royal religion. Maybe all the kings build temples, and all the gods like temples, but not this God and therefore not this king. David is not permitted to act like people in his role act.[15]

The denial of David's idea to build a house for God is not where this passage ends. Instead, we learn of the "house" that God is going to build for David.

> "Moreover the LORD declares to you that the LORD will make you a house. When your days are fulfilled and you lie down with your ancestors, I will raise up your offspring after you, who shall come forth from your body, and I will

---

14. My literal translation of 2 Sam 7:5, with emphasis on the pronouns.

15. Brueggemann, *David's Truth,* 73.

> establish his kingdom. He shall build a house for my name, and I will establish the throne of his kingdom forever. I will be a father to him, and he shall be a son to me."
>
> (2 Sam 7:11b–14a)

The first thing to note about God's promise to David is it is the promise of a house (Heb.: *byt*). We remember that David's idea was to build a "house" (*byt*)—meaning temple—for God, but God did not want that. Rather, here we see God promise to build a "house" (*byt*)—meaning dynasty—for David. The reversal here seems to suggest something that David needs to learn. It is not about what David can do for God, but about what God can do for David. The second thing to note about God's promise to David is that it sounds surprisingly similar to God's promise to Abraham, who was also promised offspring who shall come forth from his own body (Gen 15:4). In many ways then, the promise to David can thus be seen as fulfilling the promises made to Abraham.[16] A third thing to note about this promise is that the focus of the promise is not on David at all, but his unnamed son. *He* will build a house for God. *His* throne will be established forever. God will be a father to *him*. *He* will be a son to God. Although this is the high moment in David's life, David is virtually erased from this promise. The promise has an entirely forward-focusing trajectory. It seems important that even in this moment of God's greatest commitment to David, that God is also distancing himself from David. The emphasis is on God's commitment and on David's unnamed son, not on David himself.

A final thing to note about this promise is that it sets up the concept of divine sonship for the Davidic line. It is impossible to overstate how important the concept of divine

---

16. Gordon, *Samuel*, 239. Cf. Firth, *Samuel*, 385.

sonship is in biblical literature.¹⁷ It will become a way that the Psalms talk about the king of Israel (e.g., Psa 2:7). It will be a significant concept for the New Testament authors in understanding Jesus (e.g., Mark 1:11–12). The language of sonship also helpfully explicates God's commitment to the house of David. What does it mean to be son of God in this context? According to vv. 14–17 it means two things. First, like a father, God will discipline the house of David when it commits iniquity. Included in that discipline is the promise of "a rod such as mortals use, with blows inflicted by human beings" (2 Sam 7:14). This promise appears to anticipate the raising up of human enemies against the house of David, whether that be Jeroboam in 1 Kings 11–12 or the Babylonians in 2 Kings 24–25. Second, however, despite the discipline that is promised, God, like a father, will never take away his love from David's house (2 Sam 7:15–16). The picture that is painted is that God's relationship with David is of a different order than his relationship with Saul. Perhaps we are meant to see that if it were up to David and his household to uphold this relationship, what happened with Saul would simply repeat itself. God is taking the responsibility for this relationship on himself.¹⁸

David responds to God's promise with a question about his own identity. He says, "Who am I, O Lord GOD, and what is my house, that you have brought me thus far?" (2 Sam 7:18). On the one hand, this is an appropriately humble response to God's promise.¹⁹ On the other hand,

17. For recent work on this see Allen et al., eds, *Son of God*.

18. Brueggemann, *Samuel*, 257, says "This is a powerful, clear articulation of 'justification by grace' (Rom 3:28; Gal 2:16–21) in which the 'works' of David or Israel are not decisive. God loves unconditionally."

19. Cf. his response to Saul's proposal to give him one of his daughters (1 Sam 18:18, 23).

the question of David's identity is somewhat thematic of the entire narrative thus far. Is the narrator trying to keep this question in our mind? Should we know the answer to this question at this point? If we do not know the answer, I suggest, we at least should have been asking long before now. Perhaps we are going to learn something significant about David in this chapter.

David recognizes that he is reaping the benefits of God's commitment to him.

> "Because of your promise, and according to your own heart, you have wrought all this greatness, so that your servant may know it."
>
> (2 Sam 7:21)

Nathan's response to David's intention to build a house for God was "do all that you have in your heart" (2 Sam 7:3, my translation). Now, David recognizes that the commitment he is receiving from God is because of *God's* heart. As Craig Morrison states, "God's 'heart' has prevailed over David's 'heart.'"[20] The significance of this will be made even more clear as heart language comes up again shortly.

David exhorts God to fulfill his promise concerning David's house so that God's name will be made great forever (2 Sam 7:24–25). David appears to see that the purpose of God's commitment to David's house is to bring glory to God, not to David. Because of this promise, David says "your servant has found courage to pray this prayer to you" (2 Sam 7:27). This seemingly innocuous statement is more significant than it appears to be. Buried in the reasonable translation of the NRSV ("found courage") is the fact that the Hebrew literally says, "your servant has found his heart (*lev*)." This phrase occurs nowhere else in the Old Testament and I cannot help but think it is significant. I suggest

20. Morrison, *2 Samuel*, 103.

that this rare phrase brings us somewhat full circle in our understanding of David's heart.

We anticipated David in the promise that God would choose a man after his own heart (1 Sam 13:14). We then learned that David was the one whose heart God had approved (1 Sam 16:7, 12). David's heart has been challenged (1 Sam 25:31). Nathan thought that David's heart had the right idea (2 Sam 7:3). But now we see that David understands that his heart was not aligned with God's heart (2 Sam 7:21). Thus, when David says, "your servant has found his heart," I suggest that we see what it means to have a heart after God's (1 Sam 13:14). It does not mean to be a saint. Rather, it means to have a heart that is oriented toward God's heart and that is capable of being reoriented toward God's heart when it goes astray. We will have the opportunity to see this idea one more time in David's story, but for now, I think we have learned something profound about David, God, and the type of heart that God desires.

Consolidation Continued (2 Samuel 8–9)

This chapter is already long enough and if we were to spend much time on these chapters after our analysis of the Davidic covenant in 2 Samuel 7 it would feel too much like the "Scouring of the Shire" in *Return of the King*. It might feel like adding too much superfluous narrative after the main thing has been discussed. So I will limit my comments here to two observations. First, 2 Samuel 8 affords the opportunity to see God's faithfulness to David continued in his consolidation of his reign by his many victories over neighboring peoples. Second, the story in 2 Samuel 9 tells of the last descendant of Saul to whom David desires to "show kindness" for the sake of his friend Jonathan (2 Sam 9:1). We learn of Jonathan's son Mephibosheth, who is lame in his feet (2 Sam 9:3). David gives Mephibosheth everything that belonged to Saul's house. He brings Mephibosheth to live with him and dine at his own table and places the servant of Saul, Ziba, to work Saul's property on behalf of Mephibosheth. The narrative is clear that the purpose of this is that David desires to show kindness to Jonathan's son, but several readers suspect that David is keeping an eye on Mephibosheth. So perhaps David is still playing politics. Or, perhaps, he has a very keen eye for killing two birds with one stone and sees an opportunity where his commitment to his friend may also benefit him politically.[21]

CONCLUSION

Once Saul is out of the way and David has become king in Judah, the story is far from over. Just like there was a lot of maneuvering yet to do for Alexander Hamilton after the Revolutionary War had been won, there was a lot of consolidating that needed doing for David's fledgling rule. In these early chapters of David's reign, we see that his rule is founded on political maneuvering and divine blessing. It seems that David is always playing in two spheres, both human and divine. He enjoys unprecedented divine blessing. But he also enjoys unprecedented success in his political endeavors. Perhaps the two are related, but it is not always clear what that means.

In these early chapters of David's reign we have learned that he is capable of great political savvy but he is also capable of orienting his heart toward God. One of the phrases that people sometimes attribute to the Bible but that is nowhere stated is the sentiment that "God helps those who help themselves." Although the sentiment is profoundly unbiblical in many ways, it is hard not to see that

21. See Halbertal and Holmes, *The Beginning of Politics*, 57–59.

idea play itself out in David's life. Since we have met David he has always been advancing himself, but has also been concerned about orienting himself toward God. Perhaps that complexity is what makes David both so successful and so fascinating.

QUESTIONS FOR REFLECTION

1. What do you think of David's lament for Saul and Jonathan? Is he sincerely mourning or is he putting on a show for the crowd?
2. In the interactions between Abner, Joab, and David in 2 Samuel 2–3, whom do you trust? Does David act justly?
3. Why do you think it is important for God to hold David at arms length even while he is committing to him and his house in 2 Samuel 7?
4. What do you think about the dual characterization of David as one who is both politically savvy and spiritually sensitive?

7

HOME ALONE

2 Samuel 10–12

> *"You are the man!"*
> —Nathan[1]
>
> *"I have sinned against the LORD."*
> —David[2]

IN MY FAMILY, IT is just not Christmas without watching *Home Alone*. However, if I'm being honest, once I started watching it with my kids, I realized that there were some family dynamics in the movie that I didn't really want to promote. Somehow, I didn't notice those when I was a kid. Otherwise, it has everything you might want in a holiday family movie: hilarious hijinks, great characters, and a

---

1. 2 Sam 12:7.
2. 2 Sam 12:13.

touching message about family. Great holiday fun. There is another aspect of this movie that is also interesting, especially for our purposes; that is the growth of the main character, Kevin McCallister, during his time being home alone. When he first finds himself alone, he sees it as a holiday, a chance to get away with things he knows he is not supposed to do. However, as the movie progresses, he moves away from that attitude toward a more responsible way of living. He goes from bouncing on the bed, eating popcorn, eating junk food, and watching rubbish to buying groceries, doing the laundry, and defending his castle!

Like I tell my young son, how we behave when we are alone and think we can get away with it says a lot about who we are as people. Here we encounter perhaps the most famous (and certainly infamous) episode in David's life besides his confrontation with Goliath. In it we will see how David behaves when he is home alone.

AN AFFAIR TO REMEMBER (2 SAMUEL 11:1–5)

> In the spring of the year, the time when kings go out to battle, David sent Joab with his officers and all Israel with him; they ravaged the Ammonites, and besieged Rabbah. But David remained at Jerusalem.
>
> (2 Sam 11:1)

The setting for the David and Bathsheba affair is as described above. How one interprets this setting impacts the way one reads this entire episode. Readers have long noted that the David and Bathsheba episode contains a significant amount of ambiguity.[3] The story is told in such a way that it

---

3. See, for example, Sternberg, *Poetics of Biblical Narrative*, 186–229; and Yee, "Fraught with Background."

leaves a lot of things unsaid and the reader is left to puzzle over these gaps. Like we saw in the episode with David and Nabal, the way those gaps are filled in greatly changes the interpretation of the text. In the setting of this story, the questions are why does David stay behind in Jerusalem when Joab and the army are at war and how does that act characterize David?

It is traditional to view David as being derelict in his duty as king of Israel. After all, it appears that leading Israel in war was a primary expectation of the king (1 Sam 8:19–20; cf. 2 Sam 5:2). Furthermore, the disjunction between Joab and the army's activities and David remaining in Jerusalem draws a strong contrast between the two.[4] However, it is not absolutely necessary to view David negatively here. As several readers have pointed out, there are any number of reasons why it might be standard practice for David not to go out with the army. It may be that sending out Joab and the army and only being present when it was essential had become David's policy (cf. 2 Sam 10:6–18). It may be that he had learned the lesson of Saul that a king can be killed in battle (cf. 1 Sam 30:1–7; cf. 2 Sam 21:15–17).[5]

Perhaps the point to be made is that the context of this episode is not necessarily immediately clear. Is David neglecting his duty, being at his ease, and putting himself in a situation in which he should not have been in the first place? Or is David just going about his business? We will hold off making a judgment on this issue for the moment and return to it after we have gone through the chapter.

---

4. Cf. Sternberg, *Poetics of Biblical Narrative*, 194. See his further comments, "In contrast to the nation fighting at Rabbah, the king is leading a life of idleness in Jerusalem, taking his leisurely siesta, getting up in the evening, and strolling about on his roof" (Sternberg, *Poetics of Biblical Narrative*, 197).

5. Cf. the comments of Yee, "Fraught with Background," 242–43 and Firth, *Samuel*, 417.

> It happened, late one afternoon, when David rose from his couch and was walking about on the roof of the king's house, that he saw from the roof a woman bathing; the woman was very beautiful. David sent someone to inquire about the woman. It was reported, "This is Bathsheba daughter of Eliam, the wife of Uriah the Hittite." So David sent messengers to get her, and she came to him, and he lay with her. (Now she was purifying herself after her period.) Then she returned to her house. The woman conceived; and she sent and told David, "I am pregnant."
>
> (2 Sam 11:2–5)

We will not quote all of this episode, but the actual event of the affair is probably worth careful attention. Just as we picked up on the issue that was brought up in the first verse, about how David is characterized by *being* in Jerusalem, we face a similar issue here: how is David characterized by his *activity* in Jerusalem? If David was supposed to be at war and was not, it seems likely that the text is suggesting that David rising from his couch in the late afternoon is a picture of a king lazing about.

The next question that is often raised about this scene is who is seducing whom and why? It is sometimes suggested that Bathsheba, who is bathing on the roof, is really the one who is the active player in this scene and is the seductress.[6] While a number of these "ambiguities" or "gaps" in this story appear somewhat open-ended, I find this one hard to countenance. As a number of commentators have noticed, in this episode Bathsheba is almost entirely passive. She doesn't even function as a proper character. At this stage, she is more of a prop, being moved around by more

---

6. Even Robert Alter suggests that the text may suggest some level of opportunism on the part of Bathsheba (see Alter, *David Story*, 251).

powerful characters.[7] So seeing Bathsheba as carrying some of the blame of this episode is entirely contrary to the presentation of the narrative. This story is about what *David* did, not what Bathsheba did.

David's rape[8] of Bathsheba leads to the natural outcome of Bathsheba's pregnancy. In reality, this whole section functions as the setting of the story that follows. Although we refer to this episode as the David and Bathsheba episode, in reality, the David and Bathsheba scene is just the backdrop to the attempted cover-up, which is what the narrative focuses on.

A FAILED COVER-UP (2 SAMUEL 11:6–13)

Having just *sent* for Bathsheba, which led to her getting pregnant, David now *sends* for her husband Uriah, which will lead to his death (2 Sam 11:6). The episode with David and Uriah will take a deal more time than the episode with David and Bathsheba. What the extra time in the storytelling offers is characterization of David and Uriah, as we will see.

One of the key questions that readers often raise about this episode is, "did Uriah know?"[9] Did Uriah know about

---

7. See Berlin, *Poetics and Interpretation*, 25–27, who describes her as "a complete non-person, . . . not even a minor character, but simply part of the plot" (p. 27). For a nuanced reading of Bathsheba's character across Samuel and Kings, see Koenig, "Bathsheba."

8. In case it was not clear, I contend that what the text describes is in fact rape. When one party (David) is completely in power and the other party is narratively completely passive (Bathsheba) and has, as far as we know, no recourse to resist, that is rape. For a nuanced discussion of whether this was rape from biblical and modern definitions, see, Abasili, "Was It Rape?"

9. See Yee, "Fraught with Background," 243, who notes that "Our brilliant author never directly makes this clear." See further, Sternberg, *Poetics of Biblical Narrative*, 201–9.

David's adultery with his wife? If he did not, then his actions characterize him as someone who is ironically faithful in the presence of the faithless David. If he did know, then he is playing a dangerous game with the king. Why might we think he knows nothing of David's adultery? We might think that because we are never told that he does. Then why might we think he does know something of what David did? We might suspect that because of the degree to which Uriah countermands David's intentions.

When Uriah arrives in response to David's summons, David asks the perfunctory questions about how the war was going, and then tells Uriah to go down to his house to "wash his feet" (2 Sam 11:8). Whether this is a euphemism for sex, or just a statement to go to his own home and take his ease (which one presumes would lead to romantic time with his wife), what David intends is clear: for Uriah to go home and have sex with his wife to cover up David's adultery. In fact, by telling Uriah to go "wash" (*rachatz*) we are reminded of the thing that started this whole affair, David seeing Uriah's wife "washing" (*rachatz*).

It seems like a good plan, but it does not go as David intends. Uriah does not go home, but crashes with David's servants. David quizzes Uriah on his actions and Uriah states that he is not willing to experience the comforts of home while his brothers-in-arms and the ark of the covenant are in tents on the frontline (2 Sam 11:11).[10] David's response is to try again, but with the added help of alcohol. However, as Peter Ackroyd has memorably put it, "Uriah

10. As Sternberg, *Poetics of Biblical Narrative*, 526–27, argues, the requirement for soldiers to remain pure (Deut 23:9–14) does not require abstaining from sex, as is often assumed; instead it actually prescribes how a soldier can become clean again if they become unclean due to sexual activity (Deut 23:10–11). Instead, it may be that this was a practice that could be undertaken to signal increased dedication (see 1 Sam 21:4–5).

drunk is more pious than David sober."[11] Even in a drunken stupor, Uriah stays true to his moral commitment and does not go to his house. Here we must remind ourselves again that we do not know what Uriah knows. If he knows what has happened, then Uriah is making a statement to the king that he will not get off easy. If he does not know, then we are living in the dramatic irony that Uriah *the Hittite* is naturally a more faithful and admirable character, than David, king of Israel and chosen one of God. As in much of life, we cannot say for certain which is the case. Nevertheless, in both scenarios, the emphasis is on David's negative characterization. While the ambiguity of the narrative may mean that Uriah's motivations and actions remain questionable, the way the story is told emphasizes that the heinousness of David's motivations and actions are unquestionable.

KILLING URIAH (2 SAMUEL 11:4–27A)

Since David's plot to get Uriah to sleep with his wife was foiled by Uriah's faithfulness to his brothers-in-arms (or his desire to thwart David, if he is aware of David's actions), David resolves to plan "B": murdering Uriah. However, the manner in which he carries this out is one of the most heartless and cold betrayals in any literature, on par with Judas' kiss. He writes a letter to Joab, detailing the plan to get Uriah killed on the battlefield, and hands it to Uriah himself to carry (2 Sam 11:14–15). In other words, Uriah carries his own order of execution, not unlike Jesus Christ carrying his own cross.

While we learn of David's plan for getting Uriah killed (send him to the frontline, then pull everyone else back), we also learn that Joab apparently thought this was not a good plan. Joab follows the spirit of the command rather

11. Ackroyd, *Second Book of Samuel*, 102.

Home Alone

than the letter of it. Joab places Uriah in a place where he knows it will be the most dangerous (2 Sam 11:16). In the ensuing battle, several "servants of David" are killed, along with Uriah the Hittite (2 Sam 11:17). Presumably Joab thought that David's original plan would have shown itself to be an obvious plot against Uriah. Instead, Joab, the clever accomplice that he is, plots a way to get Uriah killed that is less obvious, but is instead more deadly and results in more men getting killed. Thus, faithful Joab has achieved David's goal, but in a way that has led to more death and destruction. As Robert Alter has noted, "the circle of lethal consequences of David's initial act spreads wider and wider."[12]

After Uriah's death, Joab sends a report to David. He gives the messenger detailed instructions that anticipate David's wrath at the news of such a loss of life. If the king gets angry, he says, inform him that Uriah the Hittite was also among the dead (2 Sam 11:18–21). Joab's messenger returns to Jerusalem and gives David his report. Rather than waiting for David to get angry he immediately adds the information of Uriah's death to the end of his report (2 Sam 11:24). David's response is to sigh and tell Joab not to worry. That is the nature of battle, sometimes the sword devours this way and sometimes that way (2 Sam 11:25). This response to the death of his own men to cover up his crime is a dark and low moment for David. They say revenge is best served cold, but David is here serving betrayal and it is as cold as it gets.

Now that Uriah is dead, David wastes no time in marrying Bathsheba, but brings her into his household as soon as she has completed the time of mourning for her husband (2 Sam 11:26–27). Although there have been all kinds of hints that raise one's suspicions that this deed might not be as secret as David would like, narratively, for the moment it

---

12. Alter, *The David Story*, 254.

seems that David has gotten away with it. Evil will out, they say, but sometimes it needs a little prophetic push.

PROPHETIC PARABLE (2 SAMUEL 11:27B—12:12)

At this point in the story we are given one completely unambiguous statement, and that is *God's* opinion of David's actions. "But the thing that David had done displeased the LORD" (2 Sam 11:27b), or, more literally, "the thing that David had done was evil in the eyes of the LORD" (my translation). Despite a lot of ambiguity in this episode, God's assessment of David's action is unequivocal. It is *evil*.

So, God sends the prophet Nathan to David. Nathan describes to David the situation of a poor man whose single beloved ewe lamb is stolen, slaughtered, and served by a wealthy neighbor (2 Sam 12:1–4). This story turns out to be a parable. And while there may be debate about exactly what each element in the parable is meant to represent, the intended effect of the parable is clear: it is meant to get David to convict himself. It is a brilliant rhetorical device, because David's reaction to this terrible story is to fly into a rage and exclaim, "As the LORD lives, the man who has done this deserves to die" (2 Sam 12:5). David has stepped into the rhetorical trap, which Nathan immediately closes with the proclamation, *"You* are the man!" (2 Sam 12:7). Like Jonah, whose concern for the wellbeing of a plant throws into sharp relief God's concern for all the human life in the city of Nineveh (see Jonah 4:6–11), David's outrage at the theft and slaughter of a ewe-lamb, throws into sharp contrast the outrage that he should feel and God does feel at the theft of Bathsheba and the slaughter of Uriah.

Nathan does more than announce David's guilt. He goes on to detail God's shock that his *faithfulness to* David is repaid with such *faithlessness by* David (2 Sam 12:7b–12).

Home Alone

The result will be that what David has done in secret will be returned on him in public.

> "Now therefore the sword shall never depart from your house. . . . I will raise up trouble against you from within your own house; and I will take your wives before your eyes, and give them to your neighbor, and he shall lie with your wives in the sight of this very sun. For you did it secretly; but I will do this thing before all Israel, and before the sun."
> (2 Sam 12:10–12)

For those who know where this story is going, the statement that "the sword shall never depart from your house" rings an ominous tone. As we will see in the next chapter, the rest of David's story can be seen as the consequences of this one fateful sin. David will never escape the shadow of this moment in his life.[13]

CONFESSIONS OF AN UNJUSTIFIED SINNER (2 SAMUEL 12:13–25)

Confronted by Nathan the prophet and his own conscience, David responds with the simple and concise statement, "I have sinned against the LORD" (2 Sam 12:13). This leaves us with another ambiguity in the text. How does this confession characterize David? On the one hand, some have noted that this simple confession of guilt reflects well on him when compared to Saul or later kings, who dissemble, or simply refuse to repent.[14] On the other hand, the terseness of David's repentance might strike the reader as not

---

13. For an excellent exposition on how this narrative effects everything that follows in David's story, see Bodner, *Rebellion of Absalom*.

14. See, e.g., P. Evans, *Samuel*, 403–5; and Bergen, *Samuel*, 373.

fitting the gravity of the sin and the moment, and may not signal actual repentance. After all, Saul uttered the words "I have sinned" twice when confronted by Samuel (1 Sam 15:24, 30). It might also be, that David's failure to mourn at the end of this episode characterizes him as someone who is cold, unfeeling, and unrepentant.[15] We are left with some degree of ambiguity as to how to judge David's response.

In response to David's repentance, Nathan states that David will not die. However, the child born of his adultery with Bathsheba will die (2 Sam 12:13b–14). While our focus in this book is the character of David, we must at least address the moral issue of seeing the punishment for David's sin being passed onto his son and what that might say about God. We start with the recognition that there is no easy answer to this question.[16] We may perhaps be helped by suggesting there is a difference between punishment and consequences.[17] However, it may be that Nathan is suggesting that David's sin is going to "pass over" David and the death of his son is the result.[18] It is hard not to see the death of the son as more than a consequence of David's sin and closer to a sacrificial and atoning death. While the Old Testament is clear on God's abhorrence of child sacrifice,[19] there is a logic within the Old Testament that makes some sense of child sacrifice. God apparently has the right to claim the life of a firstborn, though he provides a means by which

---

15. Obviously, if we take Psalm 51 into account, it drastically changes our interpretation of David's repentance. On this, see the excursus below.

16. Cf. Firth, *Samuel*, 428.

17. E.g., M. J. Evans, *Samuel*, 190; Arnold, *Samuel*, 536.

18. See McCarter, *II Samuel*, 301.

19. E.g., Lev 18:21; 20:3; Deut 12:30–31; Ps 106:36–39; Jer 19:4–5, though most of these are in the context of worshipping of other gods.

that does not have to be paid.[20] Furthermore, although the Old Testament occasionally makes clear that children should not be punished for the sins of their parents (e.g., Deut 24:16; 2 Kgs 14:6; Ezek 18:20; cf. Jer 31:30), it also does appear to make clear that the iniquity of parents will sometimes fall on their children (e.g., Exod 34:6–7; Deut 5:8–10). It is hard to read this scene and not suggest two things. First, this episode highlights what the apostle Paul says, that "the wages of sin is death" (Rom 6:23). Second, this passage seems to portray God as killing an innocent infant as part of the punishment for the father's sin. This falls into the category of the most difficult things to accept about God's actions in the Old Testament. There are many attempts to wrestle with these kinds of issues in the Old Testament,[21] but I have always been partial to Christopher Wright's perspective. He states, "[t]here is something about this part of our Bible that I have to include in my basket of things I don't understand about God and his ways."[22] What is apparent is that God's action here upholds the seriousness of David's sin, while also upholding his commitment to David and his line (2 Samuel 7).

The rest of this section is David's reaction to the news. The child born to David and Bathsheba is struck ill and David responds by fasting and laying on the ground all night, ignoring all attempts to get him to eat (2 Sam 12:16–17). Some have said that this looks like mourning, and that is true. However, David's response after the child dies also

20. Cf. Abraham and Isaac, Genesis 22; and the law of the redemption of the firstborn, Exod 13:13–16; 34:19–20; Num 18:15–16. On this issue, see the provocative study of Jon Levenson, *Death and Resurrection of the Beloved Son*.

21. See Lamb, *God Behaving Badly* and Seibert, *Disturbing Divine Behavior,* for two examples.

22. Wright, *The God I Don't Understand*, 86. He is talking specifically about the Canaanite conquest, but I think it applies here.

suggests that it is supplication on behalf of his dying child. Either way, what we see here is David being more intimately, and probably emotionally, involved than he was in his confession. David's initial confession, though it may have been sincere, was a little terse and perhaps perfunctory. Here, however, we see him dedicating himself to intense supplication for his child who is suffering because of his sins. Perhaps, we are allowed to see in this, some growth in David's character.[23]

Seven days after the child has died, David washes, worships, and eats (2 Sam 12:20). His servants, who, like the reader, are a bit shocked by the contrast between his behavior after the child has died and his behavior when he was sick, ask how he can go about his business like this after the child had died. David responds that while the child lived, perhaps God would spare him, but now that he has died, there is nothing he can do, "I shall go to him, but he will not return to me" (2 Sam 12:22–23).

Does David lack remorse for the child who has died? Or, has David recognized that since his supplications were not successful, he must accept God's actions with submission? We are not told outright. However, given the intensity of David's initial response, I am inclined to think the latter is more likely. In the previous chapter, we discussed how David learned about the significance of submission to the divine will. Here, it seems, he is perhaps learning that lesson again. This time as a result of his own sin.

The episode ends with David consoling Bathsheba (now his wife) and the narration of the birth of their next child, Solomon. The surprising piece of information that is given with this announcement is the fact that the LORD is said to love this son (2 Sam 12:24). It may be that this notice

23. On this reading, see Jacobs, "The Death of David's Son by Bathsheba."

communicates to us God's disparity and arbitrariness in his treatment of David's sons. One is killed, one is loved. However, it may be that what is signaled here is that God and David have moved through this dark narrative moment through the birth of this new son. It is a surprising note that will not be relevant again for quite some time. Solomon will not be a player in the Book of Samuel, but once we get to the opening chapter of Kings, this statement about God's love of Solomon may prove to be very important.

THE AMMONITE FRAME (2 SAMUEL 10 & 12:26–31)

With the birth of David and Bathsheba's son Solomon, the final paragraph of this chapter feels like a perfunctory epilogue. Joab continued the assault on Rabbah, the Ammonite town, and David went out just as they took the town. Thus, David conquered the city and returned to Jerusalem. ... The end. However, this final notice of the conclusion of the assault on Rabbah might be a bit more important than it seems at first glance.

What we have not talked about in this chapter on David, Uriah, and Bathsheba, is that their story in 2 Samuel 11 is preceded by 2 Samuel 10; an ingenious insight, I know. But 2 Samuel 10 details the Ammonites dealing in bad faith with David's servants (2 Sam 10:1–6), and Joab's brilliant military exploits against the Ammonites and their Aramean allies (2 Sam 10:7–19). Thus, the episode of David's affair with Bathsheba and murder of Uriah is framed by military action against the Ammonites. Why does that matter? Old Testament narrative often uses this bookending technique, called "inclusion," to structure a narrative.[24] One reason to frame a narrative like this is to help draw

24. On this feature, see Walsh, *Old Testament Narrative*, 109–11.

significant attention to aspects of the narrative that are contained within the frame.

In the final paragraph of 2 Samuel 12, as Joab is carrying out the assault on the Ammonite town Rabbah, he sends a messenger to David and tells him that he had better get out there otherwise Joab will get the credit for the victory rather than David (2 Sam 12:27–28). This message is essentially a rebuke of David. In other words, he says to David, "You'd better get out here or I will get all the credit for this." He recognizes the need for David to be seen as the military leader of Israel and is rebuking David for not actually being that. Why is this significant? Because one of the most significant gaps for interpreting this episode is how to interpret the inciting incident of David staying home in Jerusalem in 2 Samuel 11:1. The frame of Ammonite conflict and Joab's rebuke of David suggests that in staying home in 2 Samuel 11:1, David is already doing what he should not be doing, namely, neglecting the military actions of Israel. Thus, if David succumbing to temptation is because he was at the wrong place at the wrong time, it is because he put himself in the wrong place at the wrong time when he should have known better.

CONCLUSION

Like the character of Kevin McCallister, it appears that what we see in these chapters is what David will do when he is home alone. Like Kevin, he appeared to begin his time alone by doing whatever he wanted. Like Kevin, he seems to have learned a serious lesson along the way. That is really where the similarities end, however. David's actions when he is alone in Jerusalem are among the darkest moments in his story. His sexual indulgence and murderous cover-up have wide-ranging and long-lasting implications. It seems that we get to see David make sincere repentance and perhaps grow as a character in submission to God's will. However, as Nathan says to David, because of his actions, the sword will never depart from David's house (2 Sam 12:10). This prophetic utterance will become a lived reality in the coming chapters. Thus, in a very real way, the rest of David's story will be marked by these tragic and heinous events.

EXCURSUS: DAVID'S REPENTANCE AND PSALM 51

We have already discussed the challenge and possibility of bringing insights from the Book of Psalms into our understanding of David in the Book of Samuel in the excursus to chapter 4. Here, I want simply to note the potential discrepancy between the depiction of David's repentance in 2 Samuel 12 and the depiction of David's repentance in Psalm 51. On the one hand, it may be that, after reading the narrative of 2 Samuel 11–12, the David in this psalm feels unrecognizable. On the other hand, in both the narrative and the psalm the emphasis is on David's sin as against God more than as against Bathsheba and Uriah (2 Sam 12:13; Ps 51:4 ET). Thus, one could read the psalm as fitting expansion of David's confession in the narrative.

It is a valid hermeneutical decision to discount the psalm when interpreting the narrative because, after all, the psalm is not part of the narrative. It is also, however, a valid decision to interpret the narrative in light of the psalm because of the relationship between these two books within the canon of the Old Testament. James Nogalski helpfullyighlights the discrepancy between the narrative and the psalm.

> The Samuel narrative concludes ambiguously, without a clear sense of the extent to which the encounter changes David. By contrast, the psalm not only presents a contrite "David," but one who 1) plans to teach others from his mistakes (v. 15 [Eng. v.13]); 2) longs to see the joy of salvation (v. 14 [Eng. v. 12]); 3) requests wisdom (v. 8 [Eng. v. 6]) and cleansing from God (v. 9–11 [Eng. vv. 7–9]); and 4) knows that internal change transcends external change (v. 18 [Eng. vv. 16–17]).[25]

If we are to read the psalm as a legitimate expansion of David's confession in the narrative, we must ask why the narrative would be so terse and ambiguous with David's confession. The answer must be that the Samuel narrative is continuing to be opaque in allowing the reader insight into David's character and perhaps to allow the narrative to show that David's real turning point is after the death of the child, where he becomes emotionally involved, rather than at his confrontation, where he appears minimally remorseful of his actions.

QUESTIONS FOR REFLECTION

1. How do you interpret David's action of staying home in Jerusalem while Joab and the army are at war? Does that affect how you interpret the whole episode?
2. Why do you think this story is told in such a way as to include numerous narrative ambiguities? How does that affect the experience of this story?
3. Are you convinced by David's repentance? Is it authentic? or could it just be posturing?

---

25. Nogalski, "Reading David in the Psalms," 177–78.

4. In your opinion, does the David you see reflected in 2 Samuel 11–12 match the voice that you see in Psalm 51? What is the significance of that?

8

FAMILY MATTERS
2 Samuel 13–20

"Now therefore the sword shall never depart from your house, for you have despised me."
—God[1]

"O my son Absalom, my son, my son Absalom! Would I had died instead of you, O Absalom, my son, my son!"
—David[2]

WHEN I TEACH MY students this portion of the narrative of David's story, I always open by asking them this question: When I put the kettle on the stove, why does the water boil? Now, I teach at a university with a strong emphasis on STEM majors, so my classes are always full of Engineers

1. 2 Sam 12:10.
2. 2 Sam 18:33.

and other STEM-focused students. So, I regularly get responses about the transfer of heat from the flame to the water. Sometimes students explain something about the laws of thermodynamics. My response is to tell them that they are all wrong. The water boils because I want a cup of coffee. It is meant to be a funny icebreaker, but it illustrates an important point. Causes are complicated and we can explain the cause of things in multiple ways and see that things have a different range of causes. Yes, on one level, the water is boiling because of the physics of heat and water. However, on another level, there is a personal explanation that involves an agent, me, wanting hot water for coffee.[3] When it comes to biblical narrative, as we will see below, the issue of causation is often complicated. What we will see is what some scholars have called "dual causality."[4] Dual causality, like it sounds, is when causality is attributable to two different sources. In the case of this story, we will see causes are clearly attributable to human motivations but are also attributable to God and his intentions.

The present chapter is covering the largest amount of biblical narrative of any chapter in this book so far. This means that we will attempt to take something of a bird's eye view. This approach is important because it will help us see how this section of the narrative as a whole is the outworking of two key moments in David's life. The first is God's commitment to David. He promises David that he is committed to his line and that he will establish his dynastic throne forever. Though he may punish his descendants, he will never take his "steadfast love" from them (2 Sam 7:12–16). The second is David's actions with Bathsheba and Uriah and God's subsequent pronouncement that "the sword shall

---

3. This example is taken from John Lennox, who uses it in a number of places in the context of explaining God as the ultimate cause of the universe. See Lennox, *Can Science Explain Everything?* 36.

4. See Amit, "The Dual Causality Principle."

never depart from your house" (2 Sam 12:10). God's commitment to David and his house is clear, but God's promise that the sword will never depart David's house and enemies shall arise from within his own house dominate this section of narrative.

David does not take center stage at this point in the story to the degree that he has up to now. It appears that his family matters more than he does at the moment. As this story unfolds we will see that the overarching tone of this section is one of tragedy. It is national tragedy, but, as we will see, for David, it is intensely personal tragedy.

LIKE FATHER, LIKE SONS (2 SAMUEL 13)

Unfortunately, the worst event in David's story (2 Samuel 11–12) is immediately followed by a similarly horrible event. David's eldest son, Amnon, falls in "love" with Tamar, his half-sister (2 Sam 13:1). However, as the narrative will play out it is difficult to see anything that we might identify as "love" in Amnon's actions towards Tamar. Instead, with the help of his seemingly shady friend Jonadab, he comes up with a plan to get her alone by feigning an illness and asking his father David to allow Tamar to act as his nurse (2 Sam 13:3–6). Presumably, this sounds an innocent enough request and David allows it. Nothing is innocent here, however. When Tamar comes alone to serve the supposedly sick Amnon, he grabs her and says, "Come lie, with me, my sister" (2 Sam 13:11). Her response is one of shock and repulsion, saying that such a thing is not done in Israel (2 Sam 13:12). However, she proposes that Amnon should ask David for her hand because he will surely allow it and then all will be well in the kingdom.[5] It is not clear whether

---

5. It is not clear what to make of Tamar's suggestion. On the one hand, there is prohibition in biblical law against incest (Lev 18:9, 11; 20:17; Deut 27:22). On the other hand, there is nothing within the

this is just a tactic to put Amnon off or she was really open to marrying him if it was done properly.

The narrator is pulling no punches in describing this assault and rape. This is a repeat of David's actions with Bathsheba, with an extra emphasis on the innocence of the victim and the violence of the perpetrator. Amnon has outdone his father in terms of sexual assault. After raping her, he "was seized with a very great loathing for her" (2 Sam 13:15). He then sends her out of his room and bolts the door after her. Amnon could win awards for most horrible human being.[6]

Tamar goes into mourning and her brother Absalom comes upon her. He can see something is wrong, but he also seems to know more about the situation than one might assume. He says to her, "Has Amnon your brother been with you? Be quiet for now, my sister; he is your brother; do not take this to heart" (2 Sam 13:20). How is one to interpret Absalom's actions toward Tamar? Is he a dutiful brother outraged by the injustice that has been done against his sister? Or, is Absalom a scheming prince who sees an

---

narrative of 1–2 Samuel that suggests this would have been frowned upon and Tamar's suggestion implies that there was nothing untoward in the proposal. Is this a criticism of David's reign, that activity that goes against biblical law is commonplace? Is it an example that biblical law, as we know it, was not known to the characters of the story? Is Tamar just lying to Amnon to try to get out of this situation? It is difficult to know how to assess this reference. For various takes on this, see McCarter, *II Samuel*, 323–24.

6. Amnon actions here even exceed Shechem's rape of Dinah, the daughter of Jacob, in Genesis 34. Shechem, the Hivite(!), at least wanted to marry Dinah after raping her, which is the morally right thing to do according to biblical ethics (see Deut 22:28–29). Amnon loathes Tamar after raping her. Interestingly, Dinah's brothers avenge her rape by killing Shechem and all the males in his city, while her father, Jacob, does nothing. We will see a similar dynamic in Tamar's case, where it is her brother who will avenger her while her father does nothing.

opportunity to make a move against his brother, the crown prince? That he is a man with a plan will become apparent shortly.

The response of David and Absalom to this horrible event is important. David does nothing and Absalom does nothing. However, each character's "nothing" characterizes them very differently. David becomes angry, but does not punish Amnon (2 Sam 13:21). His refusal to do anything smacks of an unwillingness to punish his eldest son. In fact, the NRSV includes in the text, "he became very angry, but he would not punish his son Amnon, *because he loved him, for he was his firstborn.*"[7] Somehow David deems punishment of his son impossible, even in the face of his son's horrible rape of his daughter. It seems likely that we are meant to be critical of David's inaction. However, I confess, as a father, I cannot fathom facing this crisis and cannot comprehend how I would respond to it. Doing nothing, though, cannot be the answer and the narrative seems to be leading us toward that way of thinking.

Absalom did nothing in response to the rape of his sister . . . at first. He bides his time and two full years later plans a party with all the sons of David, Amnon specifically included (2 Sam 13:23–26). Absalom has an ulterior motive for this feast: the murder of Amnon (2 Sam 13:28). Once Amnon was drunk, Absalom's servants strike him down and kill him, just as he had commanded (2 Sam 13:28–29).

In the immediate aftermath of the killing, an erroneous report reaches David that Absalom had killed all of his sons (2 Sam 13:30). How this rumor reaches David, we are not told, but he is understandably devastated, tearing his garments and falling to the ground (2 Sam 13:31). In the

---

7. NRSV 2 Sam 13:21. Italics marks text not in the Hebrew text of the Masoretic Tradition (MT), but present in the Septuagint and possibly the Dead Sea Scroll manuscript 4QSam^a, though it is not extant and this point.

midst of his mourning, however, a familiar character steps in and corrects David's misunderstanding of the situation. Jonadab, who had advised Amnon to play sick in the first place, says to David that not all his sons are dead, just Amnon. As he says, "This has been determined by Absalom from the day Amnon raped his sister Tamar" (2 Sam 13:32). We are not told how Jonadab has this information, but it is highly suspicious. Are we to think that Jonadab is now a confidant of Absalom? If so, then perhaps this is evidence that Absalom was scheming from the beginning and that Jonadab's advice to Amnon was a set-up.[8] Or, is Jonadab simply a picture of a "wise man" (2 Sam 13:3) who is able to read the situation?[9] If this is the case, then perhaps the character of Jonadab functions as a criticism on David, who should have anticipated this situation and his inability to show discernment has led to another tragic event in his household.

Jonadab's insight is confirmed as David's sons arrive and Absalom flees to seek asylum with the king of Geshur. The final statement in this chapter is textually complicated. It seems it can be taken in two ways. The NRSV interprets the verse as "the heart of the king went out, yearning for Absalom; for he was now consoled over the death of Amnon" (2 Sam 13:39). Alternatively, it could be rendered with Robert Alter as, "David's urge to sally forth against Absalom was spent."[10] The difference between the two, in terms of the characterization of David, is significant. Is David longing for Absalom, as in the former option? Or, has David merely burned up his desire to go after Absalom, as in the latter? On balance, the latter option seems to have better textual

---

8. See Hill, "A Jonadab Connection."
9. Cf. Firth, *Samuel*, 439–40.
10. Alter, *The David Story*, 274.

support and makes a lot of sense in the narrative.[11] This means that the chapter ends with David either pining for his son, Absalom, or simply resolved not to pursue action against Absalom any longer. David seems clearly emotional at the end of this episode, but the object of those emotions are not always clear. He clearly mourns Amnon (and refused to punish him!), but his feelings toward Absalom are somewhat opaque.

WORDS WITH A WISE WOMAN (2 SAMUEL 14)

The next chapter begins with this insight from Joab's perspective: "Now Joab son of Zeruiah perceived that the king's mind was on Absalom" (2 Sam 14:1). More literally, this could be translated that "the *heart* of the king was on Absalom." We noted that at the end of chapter 13 it appears that David's mind was on Absalom, but whether that was longing for him or being resigned not to pursue him was not entirely clear. Here, we now get Joab's perspective on the situation and it is similarly ambiguous. David's heart is "on Absalom." This phrase could mean that David was thinking about Absalom longingly, or it could mean that David's heart was *against* Absalom. So, this chapter *starts* with an emphasis on David's focus on his son, but it also leaves it ambiguous as to what that focus is.

Joab elicits the help of a wise woman from Tekoa to tell David a story that moves him to be sympathetic to the plight of the woman's son. She then uses this to convince David to be gracious toward his own son, Absalom. David immediately perceives that Joab is behind this, which the woman confirms. He concedes to Joab's plans and allows

11. Cf. Bodner, *Rebellion of Absalom*, 46. For discussion see Tsumura, *Second Book of Samuel*, 214–15; Auld, *Samuel*, 488; McCarter, *II Samuel*, 338.

him to bring Absalom back to Jerusalem, but he is not to come into the king's presence.

For the second time, David has convicted himself by being fooled by another's story (cf. 2 Samuel 12). David, who has been no stranger to deception (cf. 1 Samuel 21; 28; 2 Samuel 11) now appears to be playing the dupe and is susceptible to others' schemes and plans. This issue is potentially exacerbated by the comments of the wise woman who twice extols David's wisdom (2 Sam 14:17, 20) in such a way that we may be a little suspicious that this is mere flattery, and we, the reader, are meant to question David's wisdom.[12]

Absalom's return to Jerusalem now secured, the narrative gives us a surprising and, it will turn out, potentially significant interlude about his good looks. Absalom is apparently uncommonly beautiful and his most significant feature is his weighty hair. He would only cut his hair once a year and weigh it, presumably to show how impressively heavy it was (2 Sam 14:25–26). Beauty plays a significant role in biblical narrative, especially in Samuel. When a character's physical appearance is mentioned, which is rare, it seems always to be narratively significant. We are thus on the lookout for the significance of Absalom's beauty.[13]

After some fireworks between Joab and Absalom, the chapter ends with Joab facilitating a reconciliation between David and Absalom. Absalom prostrates himself before David and David kisses him (2 Sam 14:33). It seems David and his son have reconciled. However, we are left wondering if everything really is well in David's household. Spoiler alert: it is not.

---

12. Cf. Miller, *A King and a Fool*, 123–24, who reads these statements as ironic.

13. On the issue of Absalom's beauty, see Avioz, "The Motif of Beauty," 351–52.

A REBEL WITH(OUT) A CAUSE? (2 SAMUEL 15–19)

Cause for a King (2 Samuel 15:1–12)

David and Absalom are now at least nominally reconciled. Absalom is living back in Jerusalem. What he does is a little ominous. He gets himself a chariot, horses, and fifty men to run ahead of him (2 Sam 15:1). This action alludes to Samuel's warning of what a king would do (1 Sam 8:11). By implication, then, Absalom's action here implies not only his royal aspirations but suggests that, "if Absalom were to be king, tyranny would result."[14] So the first narrative warning shot about Absalom and his royal aspirations has been fired.

In addition to his propensity to royal chariot rides, we learn that Absalom would go and stand by the gate and hear the people's judicial complaints. Hearing their complaints, he would sympathetically respond, "If only I were judge in the land! Then all who had a suit or cause might come to me, and I would give them justice" (2 Sam 15:4). How are we to understand this claim? Is Absalom legitimately lamenting about the lack of justice under David's rule?[15] Or, is Absalom playing politician and making promises he knows cannot be kept because he understands that just promising the people what they want will win their hearts?[16] The result is that Absalom certainly does win the hearts of the people (2 Sam 15:6).

After four years of this activity, Absalom makes his next move. He approaches David and asks him if he may go to Hebron to fulfill a vow he has made to God. David's

---

14. Bodner, *Rebellion of Absalom*, 58.

15. So Amit, "Absalom: Warrior for Justice," 265–66; and Smith, *Fate of Justice and Righteousness*, 180–82.

16. So Bodner, *Rebellion of Absalom*, 59.

response to him is, "Go in peace" (2 Sam 15:9). Ironically, this is the last thing that David will say directly to Absalom and his going will result in anything but peace for quite some time.[17] It will turn out that David's acquiescence to Absalom's request is another example of David being duped by Absalom. Just as Absalom's request for a feast with his brothers was a ploy that ended in disaster, so Absalom's request to go to Hebron will end in disaster for David. Absalom's secret intention was to declare himself king in Hebron where his father had also been declared king (2 Sam 2:1–4; 5:3). The situation does not bode well for David.

David's Exile (2 Samuel 15:13—16:14)

Upon hearing of his son's declaration of kingship, David's response is to flee with his whole household (2 Sam 15:14–18). David has been characterized by inaction for a considerable amount of the recent narrative. Now, however, he springs to action and initiates a flurry of commands leading up to his departure. And so David departs with his whole retinue, with one glaring exception. He leaves behind ten concubines to "look after the house" (2 Sam 15:16). This decision will not turn out well for these unfortunate concubines and is another sad case where women become pawns in the political machinations of those in power. Something that has been all too familiar in David's story.

From here David's story takes on the form of a travel narrative as David is exiled into the wilderness. This recalls aspects of Israel's wandering in the wilderness and foreshadows Israel's own exile from the land. Along the way, David encounters various characters, most of whom proclaim their loyalty to him. First, he meets Ittai the Gittite, who declares his utter devotion for David (2 Sam 15:21) and is

---

17. Cf. Firth, *Samuel*, 455.

accepted into David's retinue. Then he meets Abiathar and Zadok, two Levites who are bringing the ark of the covenant. David commands them to take the ark back to the city in the hope that God will eventually bring David back (2 Sam 15:25). He also sets up these Levites and their sons as spies (2 Sam 15:27). Then David encounters Hushai the Archite, whom he sends to Absalom to function as counter-counsel for Absalom. Hoping that he will frustrate the plans of Absalom's famous counselor, Ahithophel (2 Sam 15:34). David next meets Ziba, servant of Mephibosheth, who appears to be loyal when Mephibosheth is not and David promises to give him Mephibosheth's property (2 Sam 16:1–4).

Finally, David meets Shimei son of Gera of the house of Saul, who comes out cursing David as a murderer and scoundrel, claiming that God is paying David back for his crimes against the house of Saul (2 Sam 16:7–8). Rather than rebuking him, or having him killed, as his nephew Abishai suggests (2 Sam 16:9), David lets Shimei's curses stand. He appears to accept that God may have sent Shimei to curse him legitimately for his misdeeds. David hopes that it "may be that the Lord will look on my distress, and the Lord will repay me with good for this cursing of me today" (2 Sam 16:12). Though David has done little to commend himself for quite some time, perhaps he still retains some theological insight.

The possibility of David's theological insight is increased when it is noticed that in the midst of the narrative of David meeting various people in his exile, is a brief note about David's prayer.

> But David went up the ascent of the Mount of Olives, weeping as he went, with his head covered and walking barefoot; and all the people who were with him covered their heads and went up, weeping as they went. David was told

Family Matters

> that Ahithophel was among the conspirators with Absalom. And David said, "O LORD, I pray you, turn the counsel of Ahithophel into foolishness."
>
> (2 Sam 15:30–31)

A Christian reader will probably hear foreshadowing of Jesus' famous moment weeping and praying on the Mount of Olives before the crucifixion.[18] It is probably not insignificant that at David's lowest point, he ascends to a high point and prays.[19] Perhaps we are invited to see that David is finding his way again. David's story has thus far suggested that David is at his best when he is dependent upon his God. His story has brought him very low. Perhaps, we are allowed to begin to see David returning to the dependence that he learned when God promised him a dynasty (see 2 Sam 7:27).[20]

What You Did in Secret . . . (2 Samuel 16:15–23)

After David's flight from Jerusalem, Absalom and his people enter Jerusalem. Hushai the Archite approaches him and says, "Long live the king" (2 Sam 16:16). We, the reader, appreciate the double-speak in Hushai's address as we know who Hushai means by "the king" and it is not Absalom. Having taken Jerusalem, Absalom turns to his counselor, Ahithophel, and asks his advice as to what he should do next. Ahithophel, whose advice was considered to be so good it was like consulting an oracle of God (2 Sam 16:23),

---

18. Matt 26:30–46; Mark 14:26–42; Luke 22:39–46. On the way David's story connects with Jesus' story, see Daly-Denton, "David in the Gospels."

19. Cf. Bodner, *Rebellion of Absalom*, 68.

20. In an insightful study Mann, *Run, David, Run!*, 99, calls this a "turning point in this story."

advises Absalom to sexually claim David's concubines who remained in Jerusalem. That way, he says, all Israel will know "that you have made yourself odious to your father, and the hands of all who are with you will be strengthened" (2 Sam 16:21). So that is exactly what they do. They set up a tent for Absalom to have sex with his father's concubines "in the sight of all Israel" (2 Sam 16:22). The advice is from Ahithophel and has a clear political motivation and rationale. Nevertheless, we cannot help but hear Nathan's proclamation to David in the background: "For you did it secretly; but I will do this thing before all Israel, and before the sun" (2 Sam 12:12). Dual causality has come into play.

From Dupe to Deceiver (2 Samuel 17:1–22)

After advising sexual conquest in the previous chapter, Ahithophel advises Absalom to attack David and his camp immediately while they are "weary and discouraged" (2 Sam 17:2). All they need do, Ahithophel says, is kill the king and the whole conflict is over. This time Absalom decides to ask for a second opinion and Hushai is brought forward. In a rhetorically brilliant speech, Hushai counters Ahithophel's advice.[21] Using David's reputation as a fierce warrior, he plants seeds of fear into Absalom and cautions against attacking David now when he is desperate "like a bear robbed of her cubs" (2 Sam 17:8). Rather, he says, wait until all Israel can be gathered so that Absalom can overwhelm David and his band. Perhaps hindsight is twenty-twenty, but it seems pretty clear that Ahithophel's advice was the best advice and Hushai has brilliantly played upon David's dangerous reputation to convince Absalom and his men of a bad plan. The reason for Hushai's success is that God intended to counter Ahithophel (2 Sam 17:14). Thus,

21. For an excellent analysis of the brilliance of Hushai's speech, see Bar-Efrat, *Narrative Art*, 223–37.

we see through Hushai's advice, God answering David's prayer from the Mount of Olives (2 Sam 15:30–31). Once gain we have a human cause (Hushai's advice) intermingled with a divine cause (God's intention).

Hushai informs the two other spies, Zadok and Abiathar, about Ahithophel's advice and what Absalom has decided to do. They send Jonathan and Ahimaaz and, with some adventure, they manage to tell David what Absalom is planning (2 Sam 17:21). David continues his journey and meets more loyal people, including Barzillai the Gileadite, who will be remembered later. They bring him provisions and one gets the sense that perhaps the tide may be turning in this conflict.

Absalom! Absalom! (2 Samuel 18:1—19:15)

Having received provision and been given the time to escape immediate attack, David now musters his men and sets commanders of hundreds and thousands (2 Sam 18:2). Suddenly we recall a young David who was a very successful military commander and got his start as a commander of a thousand (1 Sam 18:13–16).

Here David appoints Joab, Abishai, and Ittai over the three groups. He gives orders to his commanders and tells them to, "Deal gently for my sake with the young man Absalom" (2 Sam 18:5). For the first time we are informed that David might be conflicted about this confrontation. Is this statement confirmation that David had previously been "pining" for Absalom (2 Sam 13:39—14:1)? Perhaps. But it is also possible that David is being characterized as someone who struggles being ruled by his emotions in relation to his children. Thus, there may be an arc to David's emotions with Absalom. First, he rages against Absalom for murdering Amnon, but that subsides in time (2 Sam 13:39), though his thoughts still center on Absalom in some way (2 Sam 14:1). He eventually reconciles with his son to some degree (2 Sam 14:33), enough that he at least desires "peace" for his son (2 Sam 15:9). Now, having lost one son to violence, he may not want to see the same thing come to Absalom. Amnon, we remember, was guilty of great violence against his half-sister and David was still distraught at his death. It is not surprising that David may still have feelings for Absalom, even though he is certainly guilty of causing strife in Israel.

Once the battle commences it appears one sided and David's men slaughter Absalom's men (2 Sam 18:7). Interestingly, we are told that "the forest claimed more victims that day than the sword" (2 Sam 18:8). While it is tempting to picture something akin to the trees destroying the Uruk-hai army after the battle of Helm's Deep in *The Two Towers*,[22] this more probably refers to the way that the forested terrain benefitted David's men, who had a history of being guerrilla fighters while they were running in the wilderness. It also foreshadows another tree that will presently play a significant part in the battle.

In what is probably one of the most bizarre scenes in all biblical narrative we read of Absalom, presumably on the run from the previously narrated defeat, riding through thick branches and getting his head caught up in branches while his mule rides on and leaves him hanging "between heaven and earth" (2 Sam 18:9). Thus, Absalom, the beautiful man with the great head of hair, gets caught up by the very hair that he was so proud of. It is hard not to read this as an example of the ironic downfall of a man who is caught up in his own vanity.[23] It is perhaps significant that

---

22. This reference from Bodner, *Rebellion of Absalom*, 92–93.

23. It is true that Absalom's head is mentioned here, not his hair (cf. Gordon, *Samuel*, 284–85 and Amit, "Absalom: Warrior for Justice," 267). However, given the narrative significance that is often

Absalom is suspended "between heaven and earth" as was his advisor Ahitophel, who hung himself (2 Sam 17:23). As we have seen, there is a thread of dual causality that runs throughout this narrative. Absalom's fate is literally caught between heaven (divine causation) and earth (human causation). Finally, since a mule can be a royal animal (cf. 2 Sam 13:39), it is possible to see symbolic significance in the mule riding away from Absalom. Absalom is caught by heaven and earth while he watches his royal aspirations just walk away.[24]

Unfortunately for Absalom, the servants of David find him. They seem to be concerned about David's request to deal gently with Absalom (2 Sam 18:12), but Joab has no such compunction. He stabs three spears into Absalom's heart and Joab's armor bearers finish him off (2 Sam 18:14–15). There is no gentleness displayed here and Absalom's story ends in ignominy.

After some discussion about who will carry this news to David (2 Sam 18:19–27), the news finally reaches David about the events of the battle. David's response is an emotional outcry.

> "O my son Absalom, my son, my son Absalom! Would I had died instead of you, O Absalom, my son, my son!"
>
> (2 Sam 18:33)

This repetitive outcry shows a father who seems to be distraught to the point of incoherence. This appears to be David at his most human; as Paul Borgman has stated, "here is

---

attached to physical description, it seems that a very good case can be made that we are meant to recall Absalom's great opinion of his hair here (cf. Avioz, "The Motif of Beauty," 351–52).

24. Bodner, *Rebellion of Absalom*, 95.

a real father, here is real grief."[25] Once again, in this section of the narrative, the sins of one of David's sons has led to their death and David's grief. This is a tragic human pattern in David's story that is predicated on the sins of David's family, starting with his own. However, we still cannot escape the divine cause that seems to lurk in the background of all of this: "the sword shall never depart from your house . . . I will raise up trouble against you from within your own house" (2 Sam 12:10–11).

David is not left alone to his grief, however. Joab accuses David of shaming his officers, his sons, his daughters, and his wives, all those who sided with him (2 Sam 19:5). Scolding David, he tells him to address the troops in order to rally morale for a victorious army that now feels as though they have been defeated. Joab's criticism of David is probably both harsh and wise. As Paul Borgman has noted "[w]hat threatens David's rule as King is the indulgence of David the private man."[26] It is not clear that we are to think that the cold and calculating justice of Joab is to be preferred. Nevertheless, David's personal grief, with which the reader can greatly empathize, runs the risk of damaging his hard-fought rule. David, it appears, is incapable of addressing the troops and rallying morale as Joab suggested. However, he does at least take his seat at the gate and appears publicly. It is not quite what Joab suggested but it is likely all that the king can manage in his state.

Aftermath (2 Samuel 19:16–43)

On his *flight from* Jerusalem David met a whole cast of characters, most of them friends. Now, on his *return to* Jerusalem, David engages with a whole cast of characters,

25. Borgman, *David, Saul, and God*, 168.
26. Borgman, *David, Saul, and God*, 172.

most of them probably enemies. Encountering Shimei, he swears an oath to him that he will not die (2 Sam 19:23). He confronts Mephibosheth, who seems not to have supported David in his cause against Absalom, though Mephibosheth blames Ziba (2 Sam 19:26–28). David appears not to care to decide and splits Mephibosheth's property with Ziba (2 Sam 19:29).[27] David intends to bless Barzillai the Gileadite for his loyalty (2 Sam 19:33), but Barzillai claims he is an old man and just wants to go home (2 Sam 19:34–37). The final note of the chapter is one that reminds us that the partisanship between Israel and Judah is still not healed with David back on the throne. David is nowhere to be seen in these closing verses and all we see is the slightly strange back and forth between the people of Israel and the people of Judah. All is still not well in David's kingdom.

THE SCOURING OF THE SHEBA (2 SAMUEL 20)

At the end of J. R. R. Tolkien's classic, *The Lord of the Rings*, after hundreds of pages of adventure, conflict, and final victory, after concluding various characters' storylines, the reader encounters a chapter titled "The Scouring of the Shire." Here, after the story is all but finished, a villain is reintroduced, a new conflict arises, and our heroes have to fight a new battle. Now, here, in David's story, after the torturous narrative of Absalom's rebellion, we are faced with the same issue. A new villain arises and a new conflict is introduced. For the purpose of this book, I will take my cue from Peter Jackson's film version of the *Lord of the Rings* and mostly skip the scouring of the shire, or in this instance, the scouring of Sheba.

---

27. The narrator does not give us much to go on. We have Ziba's word versus Mephibosheth's word.

The entire episode reads a bit like the greatest hits of 2 Samuel. A villain named Sheba rebels against David (2 Sam 20:1–4) and David sends his new general, Amasa, to deal with it. Joab does not trust Amasa, his rival general, and kills him in a way that recalls him killing another rival general (2 Sam 20:7–10a). Joab has dealings with a "wise woman" (2 Sam 20:16) that resolves the conflict, and Joab completes the military action without David ever getting involved. The reader is left wondering if all that much has changed in David's court. Has David really undergone the shift that we thought we saw in his flight from Absalom, or are things the same as they always were? We are left wondering.

CONCLUSION

The story from the rape of Tamar in 2 Samuel 13 through the rebellion of Absalom is one of the longest continuous narrative sequences in the whole Old Testament. Even the brief attention that we have given it here shows its complexity and interconnectedness. It is a masterful part of a masterful story. By way of conclusion we need to reflect on two things. How the story is characterized and how David is characterized.

The story unfolds as one of tragic consequences. David's actions against Uriah and Bathsheba seem to set up a pattern of behavior that his sons emulate. We go from one tragic and violent act to the next. As we have noted, this is a story where God is rarely mentioned, but ever present. The entire story is explainable from a human standpoint, based on human motivation and causes. Nevertheless, the hand of God is seen everywhere in the background as this story is a narrative fulfillment of God's proclamation to David through Nathan that, "the sword shall never depart from your house" (2 Sam 12:10).

David is characterized in this story by reference to his children. He starts somewhat detached. He allows things to happen around him and appears to let tragic situations and conflicts get out of control. Once Absalom has officially declared himself king, David appears to recover his initiative and begins to take control. At the low point of his flight, he even turns to God in prayer (2 Sam 15:30–31). This seems to turn the tide in his favor as his prayer is answered and from that point in the narrative onward everything happens to David's benefit. After the death of Absalom, however, David is now wracked by grief and appears unable fully to do the duty of king. He fades into the background somewhat as tension in the kingdom still appears. Though David has won the day, we are left with no happily ever after and David appears to be a mostly broken man. We are left wondering if David's story is a simple tragedy.

QUESTIONS FOR REFLECTION

1. What do you think of Absalom's characterization? Is he a warrior for justice that has gone wrong? Or, is he a conniving usurper?
2. How do you understand David's interactions with his children? Is there anything commendable in David as a father?
3. How do you conceive of David as a character in this sequence? Has he grown in any way or is he back to where he started?
4. What do you think of the concept of dual causality as a way that the Bible depicts God working in the world?

9

MAKING A LASTING IMPRESSION

2 Samuel 21–24 & 1 Kings 1–2

> "[H]e has made with me an everlasting covenant,
> ordered in all things and secure."
> "Be strong, be courageous, and keep the charge of the LORD
> your God, walking in his ways."
>
> —David[1]

> "[D]o not let his gray head go down to Sheol in peace . . .
> bring his gray head down with blood to Sheol."
>
> —also David[2]

---

1. 2 Sam 23:5 and 1 Kgs 2:2–3, respectively.
2. 1 Kgs 2:6, 9.

Making a Lasting Impression

THE NEVER-ENDING STORY

ONE OF THE PROBLEMS with interpreting biblical stories is the question of where they end. Take, for example, the book of Genesis. One of the key driving forces in the book of Genesis is God's promise to Abraham of land and descendants (Gen 12:1–4; 15:1–16; 17:1–21; 22:16–18; etc.). The book ends with Abraham's family becoming very numerous, but in the land of Egypt rather than the promised land. The end of the book is still waiting for a conclusion. The rest of the Pentateuch (Genesis through Deuteronomy) is still waiting for that ending. The people do not enter the land until the Book of Joshua. Where a given literary work in the Bible begins and ends is never really straightforward.

Perhaps we are helped in our contemporary context with the prominence of the Marvel Cinematic Universe. We understand the concept of multiple endings. By the time we have watched *Avengers: Endgame*—which must be considered an end if ever there was one—we have been watching numerous separate movies (each of which ended) about these characters. The existence of more Marvel movies after *Endgame* goes to show that when it comes to Marvel movies, the end may never really be the end.

In the case of David's story, we are faced with a similar issue. Where does David's story end? On the one hand, the story of David is found in the books of 1–2 Samuel and they end with 2 Samuel 24. So, there is a good case to be made that we ought to take the literary form of the Book of Samuel seriously and see the end of David's story there. On the other hand, David's succession and death is narrated in the first two chapters of the Book of 1 Kings. So, there is a good case to be made for seeing the end of David's story there. Which is it? Where we see the conclusion of the story has some significant bearing in how we interpret it.[3] In the case of David's story, perhaps we need to take seriously the fact that we have multiple possible endings (in the way we had multiple possible introductions) since David's story is found within the Book of Samuel, which is part of a larger literary corpus. To that end (pun intended) we will take a look at the two endings of David's story in 2 Samuel 21–24 and 1 Kings 1–2.

CHIASTIC CONCLUSION (2 SAMUEL 21–24)

Conclusion or Appendix?

The first possible conclusion to David's story is found in the strange collection of stories, poems, and lists in 2 Samuel 21–24. After reading the long and interconnected narrative of Absalom's rebellion from 2 Samuel 13–20, the reader who encounters 2 Samuel 21–24 may feel as if they have come upon a literary mess. It has, therefore, sometimes been relegated to the category of a miscellaneous appendix to the David story. The first chapters of 1 Kings appear to carry the story of David forward, whereas the stories in 2 Samuel 21–24 are not obviously connected to the narrative arc of David's story that we have been tracing.

Nevertheless, some have proposed that the final chapters of the Book of Samuel are not random or miscellaneous but function as a carefully structured and intentionally crafted conclusion to the book. One key to this insight comes from the recognition that these chapters are structured in a chiastic pattern.[4] A chiasm is a pattern of parallels that is frequently found in biblical poetry and

---

3. On the significance of various endings in the David story, see Green, *David's Capacity for Compassion*, 33–38.

4. See Firth, *1 & 2 Samuel: A Kingdom Comes*, 22–28 and Borgman, *David, Saul, and God*, 177–219.

narrative. The parallels are arranged in a A/B/C/B'/A' pattern. The structure of the conclusion of the Book of Samuel fits this pattern.

  A. Famine (2 Sam 21:1–14)
    B. Warrior Stories (2 Sam 21:15–22)
      C. A Song: For deliverance (2 Sam 22:1–51)
      C'. A Song: David's last words (2 Sam 23:1–7)
    B'. Warrior Stories (2 Sam 23:8–39)
  A'. Plague (2 Sam 24:1–25)

Recognizing this structure is one thing, knowing how to understand this conclusion is something else. However, the recognition that it is not random gives us license to pay special attention to it.

A second key insight about chapters 21–24 is that poems appear to be a significant structuring device in the Book of Samuel. Hannah's song sets up the story that will follow (1 Sam 2:1–10), David's lament for Saul and Jonathan marks the key middle point (2 Sam 1:17–27), and David's two songs mark the conclusion (2 Samuel 22; 23:1–7). This makes this section seem far from random.[5]

Songs at the Center (2 Samuel 22:1–51 and 23:1–7)

We will start at the center of this structure: the poems. The first poem in the structure is virtually identical with Psalm 18. A number of key things come to light in this poem. First, the poem begins and ends with David extolling God as his rock, his stronghold, his tower.

> "The LORD is my rock, my fortress, and my deliverer,
> my God, my rock, in whom I take refuge,

5. Cf. Firth, *1 & 2 Samuel: A Kingdom Comes*, 24.

> my shield and the horn of my salvation,
>   my stronghold and my refuge,
>   my savior; you save me from violence."
>
> (2 Sam 22:2–3)

> "The LORD lives! Blessed be my rock,
>   and exalted be my God, the rock of
>   my salvation."

> "He is a tower of salvation for his king,
>   and shows steadfast love to his anointed,
>   to David and his descendants forever."
>
> (2 Sam 22:47, 51)

The frame for this poem is David's trust and dependence upon God. This is strikingly similar to one of the themes that we have seen in his story. David is at his best when he is at his most dependent upon God, whether that is in his victory over Goliath, when he is on the run from Saul, when he recognizes he needs to follow God's plan for the temple, or when he is on the run from Absalom. The best of David is the David who depends on God as his rock and his fortress.

Second, it is clear that a major theme of this poem is God as deliverer. Examples abound of the way that David extols God as his deliverer.

> "He reached from on high, he took me,
>   he drew me out of mighty waters.
> He delivered me from my strong enemy,
>   from those who hated me;
>   for they were too mighty for me."
>
> (2 Sam 22:17–18)

Sometimes, it seems that David understands the concept of dual causality in his life. He appears to take credit for some of his acts and yet also sees God as the ultimate cause behind them.

Making a Lasting Impression

> "I consumed them; I struck them down,
>   so that they did not rise;
>   they fell under my feet.
> For you girded me with strength for the battle;
>   you made my assailants sink under me."
>   (2 Sam 22:39–40)

Third, and somewhat surprisingly, another theme of this poem is David's righteousness.

> "The LORD rewarded me according to my
>   righteousness;
>   according to the cleanness of my hands he
>   recompensed me.
> For I have kept the ways of the LORD,
>   and have not wickedly departed from my God."
>   (2 Sam 22:21–22)

Perhaps this is where the author of Kings gets his uncompromisingly positive view of David as one who kept all of God's commandments and walked after him with all his heart (1 Kgs 14:8). It was David's own perspective! In light of the narrative of David in which we have spent so much time, it is a little difficult to read the above lines with a straight face. In which story does David have clean hands? Has he not wickedly departed from his God? The narrative would take issue with this uncompromisingly positive poetic portrayal. What are we to make of this? Perhaps, this is a picture of David that has been airbrushed to present an ideal David, or perhaps this is David as he would want to be presented. Or possibly we are meant to see the irony of this claim. The David of the narrative is explicitly not innocent and has surely departed from God's ways. Perhaps, then, this presentation of David is meant to criticize David by highlighting the fact that he has not lived up to these claims.[6] However, it is possible to see here an emphasis on the ways that David *has* kept the way of the LORD. David is extolled for sparing Saul (1 Samuel 24 & 26) and David is known to repent (2 Sam 12:13). Perhaps, then, "[t]here is a positive statement about David and an ironic criticism of him."[7]

Fourth, the poem makes clear that David calls upon God for help.

> "In my distress I called upon the LORD;
>   to my God I called.
> From his temple he heard my voice,
>   and my cry came to his ears."
>
> (2 Sam 22:7)

In light of the episode of David's flight from Absalom that we read in the previous chapter, it is tempting to see here a reference to David's prayer to God from the Mount of Olives (2 Sam 15:30–31). It is clearly a cry of distress in David's low moment and it is also one that God clearly answers.

Finally, the poem highlights God's commitment to David.

> "He is a tower of salvation for his king,
>   and shows steadfast love to his anointed,
>   to David and his descendants forever."
>
> (2 Sam 22:51)

This is a theme that is picked up in the much more brief "final words" of David (see 2 Sam 23:5). Obviously, one of the most crucial moments in David's story is God's clear commitment to David and his line. This "eternal covenant" (2 Sam 23:5) makes all the difference in David's story.

---

6. Cf. Brueggemann, *David and His Theologian*, 163–64.
7. Firth, *1 & 2 Samuel*, 519.

Making a Lasting Impression

So, the two poems at the center of this structure pick up on key themes that have been developed throughout David's story. There is a certain sense in which they offer a rose-colored picture of the king. But it is also possible to see an ironic criticism in them as well.

Warrior Stories (2 Samuel 21:15–22 & 23:8–39)

When I was a kid, my mom was always trying to get me to read the Bible. Her tactic was to point me to sections of the Bible that she thought would catch my interest. The book of Judges and the stories of David's mighty men in these chapters were places where she regularly pointed me. I guess it worked. I'm still studying these stories.

In the conclusion to the Absalom episode, we saw that David was wracked with grief and had faded to the background again. Here, David is surrounded once again by stories of military prowess and heroics. True, it is not David that acts, but his men.[8] However, David seems associated once again with military victory and prowess.[9] Even though it is not clear how these stories connect to the life of David, chronologically, by placing them here in the conclusion, the reader is reminded of David's legacy of military prowess and of inspiring loyalty in his men.

In one particularly poignant story, David laments that he is thirsty and wished that he could have a drink from the well in Bethlehem, where the Philistines were currently garrisoned (2 Sam 23:15). David's famous three warriors, Josheb-basshebeth, Eleazar son of Dodo, and Shammah son of Agee, fight their way through the camp of the Philistines to draw water for David (2 Sam 23:16). David, however,

---

8. Brueggemann, *David and His Theologian*, 170, emphasizes this point.

9. Cf. Chapman, *1 Samuel as Christian Scripture*, 49.

does not drink it, but pours it out to the LORD, an act that is likely turning their military sacrifice into an act of sacred worship.[10] In this way, these narratives revitalize our image of David and put some emphasis on the best elements of him.

Tragedy at the Edges (2 Samuel 21:1–14 & 24:1–25)

The frame of our structure consists of two stories that have very similar elements.

	2 Samuel 21:1–14	2 Samuel 24:1–25
God's wrath is incurred leading to disaster	3 years of famine on the land because of Saul's action against the Gibeonites (21:1)	Anger of the LORD against Israel because of David's census (24:1) leading to 3 days of plague (24:15)
David intercedes	Sacrifice of the sons of Saul and their proper burial (21:3–14a)	David confesses his sin (24:10) and prays on behalf of the people (24:17) and erects an altar (24:18–24)
God relents	God "heeded supplications for the land" (21:14b)	God relents (24:16) and "answered his supplication for the land" (24:25)

Let us look a little more closely at the final frame narrative in 2 Samuel 24. The story starts with tension between God and David as God incites David to count the people and then holds David accountable for that action. This episode

---

10. On this, see McCarter, *II Samuel*, 496.

Making a Lasting Impression

may seem like divine entrapment. However, Joab, who is known more for being aggressively violent than theologically astute, understands that the census is a bad idea and challenges David (2 Sam 24:3).[11] David, however, calls for the census. After Joab carries it out, David recognizes his error.

> David was stricken to the heart because he had numbered the people. David said to the LORD, "I have sinned greatly in what I have done. But now, O LORD, I pray you, take away the guilt of your servant; for I have done very foolishly."
> (2 Sam 24:10)

This verse is crucial for two reasons. First, as we have seen throughout this study, there is a theme of David's heart that runs through his story. Here is the final reference to David's heart and it is referencing his contrition. David has been stricken of the heart previously when he felt guilty for cutting the edge of Saul's robe (1 Sam 24:5) and he manages to avoid having his heart stumble because of his intentions with Nabal (1 Sam 25:31). Here, David is relearning one of his greatest lessons. Significantly, he is coming to this realization *before* God punishes Israel for it. Second, here is an act of contrition that leads to David calling out to God to "take away the guilt of your servant." There is a fairly intricate interplay of God relenting from disaster and David repenting and interceding concerning the disaster of plague that he brings on Israel (2 Sam 24:11–25). David prays for the LORD to take away his guilt. The prophet Gad then tells David he has a choice of punishment: three years of famine, three months of fleeing from enemies, or three days

---

11. Exod 30:12 suggests that a census taken without proper ransom given for each individual will result in plague, so perhaps that is in view here.

of pestilence. David chooses the pestilence because rather than being in his enemies' hands, he prefers to be in God's hands, "for his mercy is great" (2 Sam 24:14). God brings a pestilence against the land, but relents from destroying Jerusalem. David prays again. This time he prays for his people because, after all, this was all his fault. Finally, the prophet informs David that he must build an altar on the threshing floor of Araunah the Jebusite, the precise spot where the angel who was bringing the plague stopped. David buys the threshing floor and offers burnt offerings. The LORD responds by averting the plague from Israel (2 Sam 24:25). And there, the Book of Samuel ends. David, who was not allowed to build the temple, builds an altar and intercedes on behalf of his people at the precise spot that later tradition will suggest Solomon's Temple will be built (1 Chr 22:1).

How are we to understand this final act in David's story? It is possible to read these stories suspiciously and see David's actions against Saul's sons in the first story as political machinations and David's actions in his census as the fault of an ambitious king.[12] However, it seems that themes of David's contrition (stricken heart), his dependence upon God, and his role as intercessor are powerful themes on which to end David's legacy. Thus, it could also be that both of these stories highlight David's role as intercessor for the people and thus "the main point of the material is not only to offer a positive, even idealized, portrait of David as king, but to underscore the sacral dimension of his kingship."[13] Perhaps then, in the Book of Samuel, David's story ends just as it began and just as it unfolded throughout—with a strong mix of the sacred and the secular.

---

12. Cf. Brueggemann, *David and His Theologian*, 170.
13. Chapman, *1 Samuel as Christian Scripture*, 48.

Making a Lasting Impression

THE DEATH OF DAVID (1 KINGS 1–2)

The second possible conclusion to David's story is found not in the Book of Samuel but in the Book of Kings. In many ways 1 Kings 1–2 follows the story that we traced in 2 Samuel 13–20 much more closely than the final chapters of 2 Samuel do. However, 1 Kings 1–2 also clearly functions as the introduction to Solomon's story and the Book of Kings as a whole. Nevertheless, the fact that David's death takes place in these chapters gives us a reason to regard them as a plausible conclusion to David's story as well.

A Game of Thrones (1 Kings 1)

At the beginning of the Book of Kings we find an elderly David who has lost a lot of his virility. His people bring him a young virgin to keep him warm in bed.[14] David here is past his prime, an old man who is a shell of his former self. It is plausible that this picture of the elderly David is what gives his son Adonijah license to declare himself king.

Adonijah is David's fourth son. He is likely David's eldest living son and the presumptive heir to the throne.[15] So when he declares himself king when his father is clearly aged and in decline, one might think he is within his rights. However, his penchant for royal chariot rides (1 Kgs 1:5), his good looks, and the way "his father had never rebuked him" (1 Kgs 1:6 NIV), all recall aspects of Amnon and Absalom's characterization. These echoes of earlier episodes and characters warn the reader that Adonijah's actions

---

14. It is plausible and frequently pointed out that this may have been a test to see if David was able to perform sexually.

15. Amnon and Absalom have both been killed and we assume that Chileab is longer alive since he is only mentioned in David's list of sons in 2 Sam 3:2–5.

might be more troubling than they appear at first blush and set him up as a second Absalom.

As a final warning, Adonijah's invite list to the enthronement party is quite suspect. Though he collaborates with Joab, David's general, Abiathar, David's priest, and *almost* all his brothers, he fails to invite the prophet Nathan, Benaiah and his warriors, or his brother Solomon. It seems that there may be a powerplay going on here. Perhaps Adonijah's assumption that he has the right to crown himself king is not as innocent as it first seems. Why leave out Solomon among all his brothers (1 Kgs 1:9) unless there was a specific reason to single him out?

In response to Adonijah's royal scheme, Nathan the prophet and Bathsheba, Solomon's mother, come up with a royal scheme of their own. With some rhetorical flair, which could be interpreted as trickery, Nathan and Bathsheba both "remind" David of his promise that Solomon would be king after him (1 Kgs 1:11–27). The reason that I put "remind" in scare quotes is that we have Nathan and Bathsheba's word that David made this promise, but nowhere do we have it confirmed by the narrator.[16] As we have said before, in biblical narrative it is generally understood that the narrator can be trusted, but a character can always lie.[17] Whether or not David actually promised Solomon the throne is never fully confirmed. After all, the last time we saw Nathan, he was giving David bad advice but also speaking the LORD's words (2 Sam 7:3–4). However, there are perhaps hints that David did make a promise to Solomon. First, we the readers know that Solomon is beloved of God (2 Sam 12:24–25). Second, the fact that Adonijah excluded

16. On the various oaths and the trouble with confirming their reference to the truth of the situation, see Bodner, *David Observed*, 153–76.

17. On this principle see Amit, *Reading Biblical Narratives*, 93–102.

only Solomon among all his brothers from his coronation party perhaps makes us suspicious that Adonijah knew of something like David's intentions for Solomon to gain the throne. We may be allowed to be sympathetic to Solomon's cause and think that Nathan and Bathsheba are not simply trying to con David, but we can never be fully sure. Thus, the succession of David's throne, like much of his life, is clouded by ambiguity. We, the readers, have to ask the question, whom do we trust?

David's response to Nathan and Bathsheba's "reminder" is to confirm their story and to swear an oath (for the second time?) that Solomon will be king after him. It seems plausible that David's confirmation of his oath could be considered proof that he had always intended Solomon for the throne. However, we must recall that David has been characterized at this point in the narrative as an elderly man past his prime. Nevertheless, this elderly David immediately launches into action and issues a flurry of commands that initiate Solomon's coronation on the spot. This man of action is reminiscent of David in his glory days of the past.

Meanwhile, at Adonijah's coronation feast, they hear the trumpet blast that announces Solomon's ascension to the throne. In the confusion, wondering what the horn signified, Jonathan son of the priest Abiathar, who had been an informant for David in Absalom's rebellion, informs them that Solomon has been crowned king. Adonijah's party guests quickly do an impression of cockroaches with the lights on and scatter. Adonijah himself flees to claim sanctuary by grasping the horns of the altar (1 Kgs 1:50).[18] Solomon is told and, for the first time in the narrative, he acts like a character in his own right and offers clemency for his brother Adonijah as long as he "proves to be a worthy

18. There is a tradition of the altar being a place of sanctuary where a person who has unintentionally killed someone may flee (see Exod 21:12–14).

man" (1 Kgs 1:52). This may seem like Solomon has built in an escape clause in his pardon of Adonijah, one that will come back to haunt Adonijah (see 1 Kgs 2:13–25).

Solomon, David's successor, is now king. All that remains to conclude David's story is to narrate his death.

Settling All Family Business (1 Kings 2)

The second chapter of the Book of Kings begins with the notice that David is about to die. Calling his son and heir, Solomon, he gives him his final charge. Here we have David's farewell address and it is as complicated and ambiguous as the man himself.

The first thing David says to his son Solomon is that he is to be faithful.

> "Be strong, be courageous, and keep the charge of the LORD your God, walking in his ways and keeping his statutes, his commandments, his ordinances, and his testimonies, as it is written in the law of Moses, so that you may prosper in all that you do and wherever you turn. Then the LORD will establish his word that he spoke concerning me: 'If your heirs take heed to their way, to walk before me in faithfulness with all their heart and with all their soul, there shall not fail you a successor on the throne of Israel.'"
>
> (1 Kgs 2:2b–4)

David begins his charge to Solomon with a call to remain faithful to the God of Israel, and this is surely significant. According to David, loyalty to God and faithfulness to his charge is the most important thing for Solomon's reign. He clearly references God's covenant with him (2 Samuel 7). Interestingly, David has made what was an unconditional promise in 2 Samuel 7, conditional ("*If* your heirs take heed"). It could be that this suggests that David

Making a Lasting Impression

understands this covenant as conditional. It also could be that this formulation emphasizes Solomon's obligation to follow the covenant, something David did not always do, which led to terrible consequences in his life.[19] So David begins his charge to Solomon by stressing the requirement of obedience.

He follows up that pious charge with a charge of brutal political maneuvering, the settling of all family business. He mentions three individuals: Joab, Barzillai, and Shimei. David encourages Solomon to show loyalty to Barzillai just as Barzillai had shown loyalty to David. However, David says that Solomon must act wisely toward Joab and Shimei and not to let their gray hair to go down to Sheol in peace (1 Kgs 2:5–6, 9). In other words, he tells Solomon, if you are wise you will arrange for Joab and Shimei to have violent deaths. Shimei was clearly an enemy of David and cursed him when he fled his son Absalom (2 Sam 16:5–13). However, David swore an oath to him that he would not die (2 Sam 19:23). Is David just trying to weasel his way out of his oath? Joab was David's most loyal (if violent!) military servant. It can be argued that even though Joab often did not obey David's commands, David benefited greatly from all of Joab's actions, even Joab's murders.

So, what do we make of this final hit list? After all, it is shocking that David's last words are death orders. It feels quite a bit like the conclusion to *The Godfather*. Michael Corleone can attend the christening of his son, just as he is ordering a hit on all his enemies. Similarly, David can command Solomon to obey the LORD and in the next breath order a hit on all of his enemies. Much has been written about David's hit list,[20] but one potential insight is that the main characteristics of Shimei and Joab have no place in

19. Cf. Wray Beal, *Kings*, 75.
20. For a helpful study, see Provan, "Why Barzillai of Gilead?"

Solomon's new kingdom. Shimei represents disloyalty and the North/South, Israel/Judah factionalism that tore the nation apart during David's life: first between the house of Saul and the house of David, then between Absalom and David. Joab represents violence, specifically vendetta violence. Neither of these two things can have a place if Solomon's kingdom is to have a chance. David, ever the brutal and realistic political player, sees that the kingdom requires the deaths of these two men and what they represent, a brutal but pragmatic final word from Israel's founding monarch.

David's death is then finally narrated.

> Then David slept with his ancestors, and was buried in the city of David. The time that David reigned over Israel was forty years; he reigned seven years in Hebron, and thirty-three years in Jerusalem.
>
> (1 Kgs 2:10–11)

This is a formal notice of David's death and it fits what would be considered a "good death" in the perspective of the Old Testament. Abraham is the paradigm example of a good death (Gen 25:7–11). In biblical tradition a character has lived a good life and has a good death if they follow the pattern set by Abraham. Recognizing this concept of an ideal death, it is clear that David dies an ideal death.[21]

Ideal Death	David's Death (1 Kings 2:10–12)
long life	Long (forty-year) reign (2:11)
dies in peace	Slept with ancestors (2:10)
progeny	Son is established on his throne (2:12)
buried in own land	Buried in city of David (2:10)

21. On the concept of the good or ideal death, see Spronk, "Good Death and Bad Death."

So, David dies in a fashion that characterizes it as a good death. His story concludes with his son on the throne, with his throne secured, and at the end of a long (if turbulent) life. Thus, David's life ends in a manner that signifies a life well-lived.

CONCLUSION

The two possible endings of David's story both emphasize different things. They both put a slightly different spin on David's life. Both, however, have significant things to suggest about David. The first ending, in 2 Samuel 21–24 emphasizes David's piety and dependence upon God in the two songs at the center of the concluding structure. It also emphasizes David's military prowess in the lists of his warriors and their famous deeds. Finally, it highlights David's relationship with God and his capacity for repentance and intercession in the famine and plague stories. The problematic aspects of David's character are still present, but his capacity for repentance and intercession highlight that, at the end of the day, David's standing with God is still good.

In the second ending, we see a slightly different emphasis. David is old and perhaps vulnerable. However, he finds a little spark again when he initiates the crowning of Solomon. Once again, the man of action comes to life in a time of crisis. His final words to Solomon feel paradigmatically David. In many ways, David's final words match his first words. We noted that in David's first speech he was characterized as being ambitious and opportunistic as well as pious for God's reputation. Here, in David's last words, he emphasizes that Solomon must remain faithful to God and his commands, but he must also be savvy and end the lives of those who represent disloyalty, factionalism, and vendetta violence. Here, David ends his public life and career the way it began. He is a man marked by faith *and* ambition, by spirituality *and* selfishness, by loyalty *and* violence. In other words, even in the conclusion of his story, David is "human, fully, four-dimensionally, recognizably human."[22]

QUESTIONS FOR REFLECTION

1. Which conclusion to David's story do you find more compelling?
2. How does the way we see David's story differ if we conclude it in Samuel or in Kings?
3. What do you think of David's last words? How do they reflect the characterization of David that we have seen throughout his story?
4. Do you think David's story is ultimately tragic or are there elements of redemption in it?

---

22. Halpern, *David's Secret Demons*, 6.

10

DAVID

A Man after God's Own Heart

DAVID: THE HUMAN

IN MANY WAYS IT can accurately be said that in David we see, "a symbol of the complexity and ambiguity of human experience itself."[1] We have come now to the end of that journey. We have seen the highs and lows of his life. We have journeyed with him from the battlefield in the Elah Valley, to his sojourn in Philistine territory, to his adulterous treachery in his Jerusalem palace, to his return to Jerusalem after his flight from Absalom.

We first encountered the idea of David. The hope for a man after God's own heart that would be a better solution than Saul. When we met him, he was a surprising choice. He didn't look like what a king was be expected to look like. He was a ruddy youth. Nevertheless, we learned that God

---

1. Frontain and Wojcik, "Transformations of the Myth of David," 5.

had judged something about his heart as worthy (1 Sam 16:7, 12). He proved himself on the battlefield, first as the slayer of Goliath (1 Samuel 17), then as a rising military commander (1 Samuel 18). Throughout his early rise, he was marked as a man of both piety and ambition. The sacred and secular dimensions were always mingled in David.

From very early on, David was a man who had a complicated relationship with the ruling house. He was loved by Jonathan and Michal, but hated by Saul. That hatred led to Saul's attempts to kill David. As a man on the run we saw David in all his complexity. On the one hand, he was capable of the deception of a priest (1 Samuel 21). On the other hand, he seemed regularly to rely on God (1 Samuel 23). He was both capable of graciously sparing the LORD's anointed (1 Samuel 24, 26) and wrathful violence against Nabal (1 Samuel 25).

In his sojourn amongst the Philistines, David was capable of great violence against the towns whom he raided and simultaneously appeared to remain loyal to God and the Israelite people. The ambiguity of David is never fully resolved, however. We never get a final answer as to what David would have done if he had been forced to face Saul in battle. God, it appears, rescues him from that choice.

We saw the David who was capable of great emotion in his lament for Saul and Jonathan. Though he lamented the deaths of Saul and Jonathan, he pressed his advantage and consolidated his power over Israel and Judah, even if his right-hand man, Joab, did most of the violent work. At the height of his power, we gained insight into God and David's relationship as God came and both reprimanded David and made unprecedented commitment to him (2 Samuel 7). He reprimanded his assumption that David's intentions would always be approved by God but he also committed to David and his house for all time.

David

This high point of David's story was followed very quickly by his low point (2 Samuel 11–12). David rose like a meteor, but he fell like Icarus. It was sudden, tragic, and his own doing. Enjoying the comforts of home while his men were at war, David was tempted first by Bathsheba, then by his desire to cover it up. Succumbing to both of those temptations led to Bathsheba's rape and Uriah's murder. The result of which was the sword never departing from David's household.

After David's sins with Bathsheba and Uriah, events spiral out of control and David becomes a victim of the consequences of his actions. Amnon rapes Tamar, Absalom murders Amnon and then rebels against David. All the while, David does very little. It is not until David is on the run from Absalom and eventually takes active steps to pray to God on the Mount of Olives and then begins to plan his defense against Absalom that David becomes an active character again. David, however, cannot escape the continued tragedy of the consequences of his actions and faces the death of his son Absalom, which all but breaks him.

The ending of David's story can be told in at least two different ways. It can be told as a collection of stories and poems that emphasize David's sins and repentance, his dependence upon God, and his military success (2 Samuel 21–24). Or, it can be told in the story of Solomon's succession, which emphasizes David's conviction that commitment to God is paramount, alongside his ruthless political savvy. Like the man himself, the ending of David's story is complicated.

In all of this, we see in David an authentic human being. At his best, he has good aspirations, seeks God's counsel, is capable of genuine relationships, and is willing to accept correction. At his worst, he is ambitious, deceptive, susceptible to temptation, and ruthless. In other words, as a true human being he has some of our greatest qualities and our worst faults. If there is something in David that is true to the human experience, then one thing we may say about the human experience is that it is inherently complex and ambiguous. As God tells Samuel, only God "looks on the heart" (1 Sam 16:7).

DAVID: A MAN AFTER GOD'S OWN HEART?

Having traveled this far on this journey, I wonder if we are not still in the same place as Nabal asking, "Who is David? Who is the son of Jesse?" (1 Sam 25:10). The approach that I want to take to answering that question is to look at the issue that we began with, namely, the reference to David's heart. Along the way we have noted various references to David's heart. If we pay careful attention to those references, and if he really is a man after God's own heart (1 Sam 13:14), then perhaps we might figure out what that means.

Before we ever met David, we were introduced to him in Samuel's prophetic word to Saul. After failing to follow through on the Lord's commands, Samuel says to Saul, "the Lord has sought out a man after his own heart; and the Lord has appointed him to be ruler over his people" (1 Sam 13:14). As the reader knows, this other man will turn out to be David. Thus, we are introduced to the *idea* of David before we are ever introduced to the person. Our expectations for him are piqued before we ever even encounter him. The expectations that we do have here are twofold. First, David is here characterized in contrast to Saul. He is being chosen because Saul had failed. Second, David is here described as having a heart that is likened unto God's in some way.[2]

---

2. We recall that many scholars do not read this passage as saying something about David's character, but rather as saying something about God's choice. For my argument about why it says something

David

Before we ever meet David, the reference to his heart raises our anticipation of a character who is a counterpoint to Saul and is aligned with God in some way.

When we finally meet David, we meet him in the context of his brothers (especially Eliab) being rejected. In that scene, we learn that "the LORD does not see as mortals see; they look on the outward appearance, but the LORD looks on the heart" (1 Sam 16:7). Since David is the one who is chosen, this implies that there is something in David's character that God approves of. He may not have the expected exterior, but he has the interior that God chooses.

David finally acts like a character in his own right once he arrives on the battlefield in the Elah Valley. In response to his first words, which were about reward and God's reputation, his brother calls him out and says, "I know the presumption and evil of your heart" (1 Sam 17:28). As we discussed when we looked at this passage, Eliab's challenge of David puts the reader in the position of knowing that Eliab is wrong about David's heart and yet, it puts the question of David's heart into the reader's mind. Do we really know what is in David's heart? Are we sure? One of the things that we highlighted in the part of the story that happens after the fight with Goliath is a section of narrative where we see the thoughts and feelings of a lot of the characters, but not the thoughts and feelings of David. This confrontation between Eliab and David set us up to be suspicious of David's heart even while we still think that he can be said to be a man after God's own heart.

Having seen the big giant and being willing to confront him, David is taken before Saul where he says, "Let no one's heart fail because of him; your servant will go and fight with this Philistine" (1 Sam 17:32). Of course, an alternative

---

about David's character, see Johnson, "The Heart of Yhwh's Chosen One."

reading is "let not my lord's heart fail." Here we see David contrasted again with Saul and the rest of the Israelite men. What is in David's heart in this instance? A willingness to take on the enemy of Israel that is not present in Saul or anyone else. David, at least, has a heart that will not fail.

After his break with Saul, David is on the run for his life. David's heart is mentioned at least two times in this part of his life. First, while David is on the run and hiding in a cave, he comes upon Saul and cuts a corner from his robe. Immediately he is "stricken to the heart" (1 Sam 24:5). One thing we learn about David's heart here is that he is capable of regretting his actions and, presumably, changing his behavior because of it (though, of course, he will do something similar again in chapter 26). Shortly after this event, David approaches Nabal asking for payment for the services his men performed for him in the wilderness. When Nabal refuses, David plans a slaughter. Before he gets there, he is confronted by Nabal's wise wife Abigail and she turns him aside from his wrath saying, "my lord shall have no cause of grief, or pangs of conscience, for having shed blood without cause" (1 Sam 25:31). As we noted above, the phrase, "pangs of conscience" more literally translated would be, "stumbling of the heart." In other words, with this reference to David's heart we learn that David is capable of taking correction *before* he goes wrong. In the previous example, he did something he regretted and was stricken in his heart. In this case, he avoids being stricken in his heart by the wisdom of another character. Although he will not always take wise advice, he is, apparently, capable of correction.[3]

---

3. We could add the reference to David's heart when he considers going over to the Philistines: "David said in his heart, 'I shall now perish one day by the hand of Saul'" (1 Sam 27:1). If we include this reference, then we add a reference to David's capacity for human fear.

David

After Saul dies in battle and David wins the war against Saul's son Ishbosheth, he arrives at his pinnacle moment. David proposes that he should build a house for God. The prophet Nathan suggests to him that he should do all that he has in his heart because God is with David (2 Sam 7:3). However, Nathan turns out to be wrong in this instance. Instead, God will build a house for David. But God means a house of human beings, a dynasty, rather than a physical house. After David takes this course-correction from the prophet, David prays, "your servant has found courage to pray this prayer to you" (2 Sam 7:27). As we noted above, the word translated "courage" is actually the word for heart. Literally, David has found his heart to pray to God. These two references to David's heart in this pivotal chapter suggest two things. First, David's heart cannot be assumed always to be aligned with God's heart. When that assumption is made, there is space for it to go wrong. Whatever the phrase "a man after [God's] own heart' (1 Sam 13:14) means, it cannot mean that David's will is always aligned with God's will. Second, we learn that upon taking correction from the prophet, David has found his heart to approach God. This, I suggest, implies that David's heart has been turned again toward God's heart. In other words, David has learned what it means to be a man after God's own heart. It means to have one's heart tuned to or inclined after God's. Accepting God's course correction and God's gracious promise to him has recalibrated David into a man after God's own heart again.

After this high point in David's life, his story takes a hard fall. Interestingly, there are only two references to David's heart in all of 2 Samuel 9–20 and both of them have the same context and both, interestingly, are from the perspective of questionable characters. In the aftermath of the connected stories of David's horrible episode of the rape of Bathsheba, the murder of Uriah, after Amnon's rape of

Tamar, and Absalom's orchestration of the murder of Amnon, David hears a rumor that all of his sons are dead and, grief-stricken, tears his garments and falls to the ground. Jonadab, Amnon's friend who concocted the plan to get Amnon alone with Tamar, tells David that it is only Amnon that is dead. "Do not let my lord the king take it to heart," he says (2 Sam 13:33). Shortly after this, Absalom has fled and Joab, David's nephew, general, and sometime hitman, "perceived that the king's heart was on Absalom" (2 Sam 14:1).[4] A couple of things are significant about these references to David's heart. First, it is not entirely clear that either Jonadab or Joab have a good sense of what is in David's heart. Jonadab's appeal to David not to "take it to heart" asks of the king something wildly out of character for him, especially in relation to his sons. Joab's perception that David's heart was on Absalom is likely true, but the reader is left unclear as to what that means. Does he desire to be reconciled to Absalom? Or, does he still harbor anger at Absalom for robbing him of his firstborn? What is clear is that during this darkest part of David's life, the only references to his heart are to describe his heart as focused on his sons. This perhaps subtly communicates that David is capable of having his heart inclined toward something other than God. And, in this case, when that happens, it marks the darkest point in his life.

Finally, we come to the conclusion of the Book of Samuel. After having been enticed to number the people, despite Joab's warnings, David realizes that what he has done was wrong. For the second time in his story David is "stricken to the heart" because of an action he has taken (2 Sam 24:10). After the long and dark narrative of the struggles in David's household, where the only references to David's heart mark his obsession with his sons, it is striking

---

4. My translation. NRSV translates heart as "mind" here.

David

that the final reference to David's heart is about his capacity for regret and repentance. In this final episode in the Book of Samuel, we see David's heart characterized as one that has the capacity for course correction.

In other words, by surveying references to David's heart, we may suggest that for David to have a heart "after [God's] own heart" means the following. It means that David has a heart that is obedient, by contrast with disobedient Saul (1 Sam 13:13–14). It means that David has a heart that is obedient, by contrast with a fearful Saul (1 Sam 17:32). It means that David has a heart that is able to be convicted of wrongdoing or intended wrongdoing (1 Sam 24:5; 25:31; 2 Sam 24:10). It means that David has a heart that is not always aligned with God (2 Sam 7:3) but is able to be realigned with God (2 Sam 7:27). We are led to be suspicious of David's heart (1 Sam 17:28). He is, after all, human, with significant human faults (cf. 2 Samuel 11). His heart also has a capacity to be focused on other things, frequently in David's case, his sons (2 Sam 13:33; 14:1). Nevertheless, the references to David's heart throughout his story seems to suggest that for David to be a "man after [God's] own heart" means that he has a heart that is aligned and capable of being realigned to God.[5]

David is far from perfect. He goes wrong. Then he goes wrong again. It is a cliché to say that David was a great sinner and a great repenter. That sentiment probably comes more from Psalm 51 than it does from David's story. However, being attentive to the flow of David's story and the references to his heart suggests that that old adage is not as far off as one might think on a cursory reading of David's story. In the climax of the 2002 film version of *The Count of*

---

5. Cf. the conclusion about God and David's relationship in Green, *David's Capacity for Compassion*, 261–62. Her subsection is titled "hearts aligned."

Monte Cristo, after Edmund has fatally stabbed Mondego, Mondego asks Edmund, "What happened to your mercy?" To which Edmund replies, "I'm a count, not a saint." We can say something similar about David. He is a man after God's heart, not a saint. God, it seems, does not require a servant who is infallible or even always admirable. Instead, if we are attentive to the theme of the heart in David's story, then the recognition that David's heart is constantly willing to be aligned and realigned with God's heart suggests that this may be exactly what it means to be a man or woman after God's own heart.

BIBLIOGRAPHY

Abasili, Alexander Izuchukwu. "Was It Rape? The David and Bathsheba Pericope Re-Examined." *VT* 61 (2001) 1–15.

Ackerman, Susan. *When Heroes Love: The Ambiguity of Eros in the Stories of Gilgamesh and David*. New York: Columbia University Press, 2005.

Ackroyd, Peter. *The Second Book of Samuel*. CBC. Cambridge: Cambridge University Press, 1977.

Alter, Robert. *The Art of Biblical Narrative*. Rev. ed. New York: Basic, 2011.

———. *The David Story: A Translation with Commentary of 1 and 2 Samuel*. New York: Norton, 1999.

Amit, Yairah. "Absalom: A Warrior for Justice—A Life Story in Seven Stages." In *Characters and Characterization in the Book of Samuel*, edited by Keith Bodner and Benjamin J. M. Johnson, 255–70. London: Bloomsbury T. & T. Clark, 2020.

———. "The Dual Causality Principle and Its Effects on Biblical Literature." *VT* 37 (1987) 385–400.

———. *Reading Biblical Narratives: Literary Criticism and the Hebrew Bible*. Minneapolis, MN: Fortress, 2001.

Arnold, Bill T. *1 & 2 Samuel*. NIVAC. Grand Rapids: Zondervan, 2003.

Athas, George. "'A Man After God's Own Heart': David and the Rhetoric of Election to Kingship." *JESOT* 2.2 (2013) 191–98.

Avioz, Michael. "The Motif of Beauty in the Books of Samuel and Kings." *VT* 59.3 (2009) 341–59.

Auerbach, Eric. "Odysseus' Scar." In *Mimesis: The Representation of Reality in Western Thought*, 3–24. Princeton, NJ: Princeton University Press, 2003.

Baden, Joel S. *The Historical David: The Real Life of an Invented Hero*. New York: HarperOne, 2013.

Bibliography

Bar-Efrat, Shimon. *Narrative Art in the Bible*. London: T. & T. Clark, 2004.

Barstad, Hans M. *History and the Hebrew Bible: Studies in Ancient Israelite and Ancient Near Eastern Historiography*. FAT 61. Tübingen: Mohr Siebeck, 2008.

Becking, Bob. "David between Ideology and Evidence." In *Between Evidence and Ideology: Essays on the History of Ancient Israel Read at the Joint Meeting of the Society for Old Testament Study and the Oud Testamentisch Werkgezelschap, Lincoln, July 2009*, edited by Bob Becking, and Lester Grabbe, 31–40. Leiden: Brill, 2011.

Becking, Bob, and Paul Sanders. "Plead for the Poor and the Widow: The Ostracon From Khirbet Qeiyafa as Expression of Social Consciousness." *ZABR* 17 (2011) 133–48.

Bergen, Robert D. *1, 2 Samuel*. NAC 7. Nashville, TN: B&H, 1996.

Bodner, Keith. *David Observed: A King in the Eyes of His Court*. HBM 5. Sheffield, UK: Sheffield Phoenix Press, 2005.

———. *The Rebellion of Absalom*. London: Routledge, 2014.

———. *1 Samuel: A Narrative Commentary*. HBM 19. Sheffield, UK: Sheffield Phoenix Press, 2009.

Bodner, Keith, and Benjamin J. M. Johnson. "David: Kaleidoscope of a King." In *Characters and Characterization in the Book of Samuel*, edited by Keith Bodner and Benjamin J. M. Johnson, 122–39. London: Bloomsbury T. & T. Clark, 2020.

Bodner, Keith and Ellen White. "Some Advantages of Recycling: The Jacob Cycle in a Later Environment." *BibInt* 22 (2014): 20–33.

Borgman, Paul. *David, Saul, & God: Rediscovering an Ancient Story*. New York: Oxford University Press, 2008.

Brueggemann, Walter. *David and His Theologian: Literary, Social, and Theological Investigations of the Early Monarchy*. Eugene, OR: Cascade, 2011.

———. *David's Truth in Israel's Imagination and Memory*. Minneapolis, MN: Fortress, 1985.

———. *First and Second Samuel*. Interpretation. Louisville, KY: John Knox Press, 1990.

Chapman, Stephen B. *1 Samuel as Christian Scripture: A Theological Commentary*. Grand Rapids: Eerdmans, 2016.

Chisholm, Robert B., Jr. "Cracks in the Foundation: Ominous Signs in the David Narrative." *BibSac* 172 (2015) 154–76.

Daly-Denton, Margaret M. "David in the Gospels." *Word & World* 23.4 (2003) 421–29.

Bibliography

Davies, Philip R. *In Search of 'Ancient Israel': A Study in Biblical Origins*. 2nd ed. London: Bloomsbury T. & T. Clark, 2015.

DeRouchie, Jason S. "The Heart of Yhwh and His Chosen One in 1 Samuel 13:14." *BBR* 24.4 (2014) 467–89.

Dever, William G. *Beyond the Texts: An Archaeological Portrait of Ancient Israel and Judah*. Atlanta: SBL, 2017.

Edelman, Diana Vikander. *King Saul in the Historiography of Judah*. JSOTSupp 121. Sheffield, UK: Sheffield Academic Press, 1991.

Esler, Philip F. "Ancient Mediterranean Monomachia in the Light of Cultural Anthropology: The Case of David and Goliath." In *The Idea of Man and Concepts of the Body: Anthropological Studies on the Ancient Cultures of Israel, Egypt, and the Near East*, edited by Anjelika Berjelung et al., 3–37. Tübingen: Mohr/Siebeck, 2011.

Evans, Mary J. *1 and 2 Samuel*. NIBC, Peabody, MA: Hendrickson, 2000.

Evans, Paul S. *1–2 Samuel*. SGBC. Grand Rapids: Zondervan, 2018.

———. "From a Head above the Rest to No Head at All: Transformations in the Life of Saul." In *Characters and Characterization in the Book of Samuel* edited by Keith Bodner and Benjamin J. M. Johnson, 101–20. London: Bloomsbury T. & T. Clark, 2020.

Firth, David G. *1 & 2 Samuel*. AOTC 8. Downers Grove, IL: InterVarsity Press, 2009.

———. *1 & 2 Samuel: An Introduction and Study Guide: A Kingdom Comes*. T. & T. Clark Study Guides to the Old Testament. London: Bloomsbury T. & T. Clark, 2017.

Frontain, Raymond-Jean, and Jan Wojcik. "Introduction: Transformations of the Myth of David." In *The David Myth in Western Literature*, edited by Raymond-Jean Frontain, and Jan Wojcik, 1–11. West Lafayette, IN: Purdue University, 1980.

Galil, Gershon. "The Hebrew Inscription From Khirbet Qeiyafa/ne☒a'Im: Script, Language, Literature, and History." *UF* 41 (2009) 193–242.

Gilmour, Rachelle. *Representing the Past: A Literary Analysis of Narrative Historiography in the Book of Samuel*. VTSupp 143. Leiden: Brill, 2011.

Goldingay, John. *Psalms 1–41*. BCOTWP. Grand Rapids: Baker Academic, 2006.

Gordon, Robert P. *I and II Samuel: A Commentary*. Exeter, UK: Paternoster, 1986.

Bibliography

Green, Barbara. *David's Capacity for Compassion: A Literary-Hermeneutical Study of 1–2 Samuel*. LHBOTS 641. London: Bloomsbury T. & T. Clark, 2017.

Greenspahn, Frederick E. *When Brothers Dwell Together: The Preeminence of Younger Siblings in the Hebrew Bible*. Oxford: Oxford University Press, 1994.

Halpern, Baruch. *David's Secret Demons: Messiah, Murderer, Traitor, King*. Grand Rapids: Eerdmans, 2001.

Hill, Andrew E. "A Jonadab Connection in the Absalom Conspiracy?" *JETS* 30 (1987) 387–90.

Jacobs, Jonathan. "The Death of David's Son By Bathsheba (II Sam 12:13–25): A Narrative in Context." *VT* 63.4 (2013) 566–76.

Johnson, Benjamin J. M. "Character as Interpretive Crux in the Book of Samuel." In *Characters and Characterization in the Book of Samuel*, edited by Keith Bodner and Benjamin J. M. Johnson, 1–13. London: Bloomsbury T. & T. Clark, 2020.

———. "David Then and Now: Double-Voiced Discourse in 1 Samuel 16:14–23." *JSOT* 38.2 (2013) 201–15.

———. "Did David Bring a Gun to a Knife Fight? Literary and Historical Considerations in Interpreting David's Victory over Goliath." *ExpT* 124.11 (2013) 530–37.

———. "The Heart of Yhwh's Chosen One in 1 Samuel." *JBL* 131.3 (2012) 455–66.

———. "Israel at the Time of the United Monarchy: David and Solomon." In *The Biblical World*, 2nd ed., edited by Katharine Dell, 498–518. London: Routledge, 2021.

———. "Making a First Impression: The Characterization of David and His Opening Words in 1 Samuel 17:25–31." *TynBul* 71.1 (2020) 75–93.

———. *Reading David and Goliath in Greek and Hebrew: A Literary Approach*. Forschungen zum Alten Testament 2. Reihe, Vol. 82. Tübingen: Mohr Siebeck, 2015.

Johnson, Vivian L. *David in Distress: His Portrait through the Historical Psalms*. LHBOTS 505. London: T. & T. Clark, 2009.

King, Philip J. "David Defeats Goliath." In *"Up to the Gates of Ekron": Essays on the Archaeology and History of the Eastern Mediterranean in Honor of Seymour Gitin*, edited by Sidnie White Crawford, 350–57. Jerusalem: The Israel Exploration Society, 2007.

Knapp, Andrew. *Royal Apologetic in the Ancient Near East*. Writings from the Ancient World Supplement Series, Vol. 4. Atlanta: SBL, 2015.

Bibliography

Koenig, Sara. "Bathsheba between the Lines and beneath the Surface." In *Characters and Characterization in the Book of Kings*, edited by Keith Bodner and Benjamin J. M. Johnson, 32–49. London: Bloomsbury T. & T. Clark, 2020.

Lamb, David T. *God Behaving Badly: Is the God of the Old Testament Angry, Sexist, and Racist?* Downers Grove, IL: IVP Books, 2011.

Lennox, John C. *Can Science Explain Everything?* N.P.: The Good Book Company, 2019.

Levenson, Jon D. "1 Samuel 25 as Literature and as History." *Catholic Biblical Quarterly* 40.1 (1978) 11–28.

———. *The Death and Resurrection of the Beloved Son: The Transformation of Child Sacrifice in Judaism and Christianity.* New Haven, CT: Yale University Press, 1993.

Linafelt, Tod. "Private Poetry and Public Eloquence in 2 Samuel 1:17–27: Hearing and Overhearing David's Lament for Jonathan and Saul." *Journal of Religion* 88.4 (2008) 497–526.

Long, V. Philips. *The Art of Biblical History.* Foundations of Contemporary Interpretation 5. Grand Rapids: Zondervan, 1994.

———. "First and Second Samuel." In *The Complete Literary Guide to the Bible*, edited by Leland Ryken and Tremper Longman III, 165–81. Grand Rapids: Zondervan, 1993.

Mann, Steven Thatcher. *Run, David, Run! An Investigation of the Theological Speech Acts of David's Departure and Return (2 Samuel 14–20).* Siphrut: Literature and Theology of the Hebrew Scriptures, Vol. 10. Winona Lake, IN: Eisenbrauns, 2013.

Mazar, Amihai. "Archaeology and the Biblical Narrative: The Case of the United Monarchy." In *One God—One Cult—One Nation: Archaeological and Biblical Perspectives*, edited by Reinhard G. Kratz, and Hermann Spieckermann, 29–58. Berlin: De Gruyter, 2010.

Mazar, Eilat. *The Palace of King David: Excavations at the Summit of the City of David Preliminary Report of Seasons 2005–2007.* Jerusalem: Shoham Academic Research and Publication, 2009.

McCarter, P. Kyle, Jr. *I Samuel: A New Translation with Introduction and Commentary.* AB. New York: Doubleday, 1980.

———. *II Samuel: A New Translation with Introduction and Commentary.* AB. New York: Doubleday, 1984.

McKenzie, Steven L. *King David: A Biography.* New York: Oxford University Press, 2000.

Meyers, Carol. "Ephod." In *ABD* 2: 550.

Bibliography

Millard, Alan. "The Armor of Goliath." In *Exploring the Longue Durée: Essays in Honor of Lawrence E. Stager*, edited by J. David Schloen, 337–43. Winona Lake, IN: Eisenbrauns, 2009.

———. "The Ostracon from the Days of David Found at Khirbet Qeiyafa." *TynBul* 62.1 (2011) 1–13.

Miller, Virginia. *A King and a Fool? The Succession Narrative as a Satire*. BINS, 179. Leiden: Brill, 2019.

Miscall, Peter D. *1 Samuel: A Literary Reading*. Bloomington, IN: Indiana University Press, 1986.

Morrison, Craig E. *2 Samuel*. Berit Olam. Collegeville, MN: Liturgical, 2013.

Noll, K. L. *The Faces of David*. JSOTSup 242. Sheffield, UK: Sheffield Academic Press, 1997.

Olyan, Saul M. "'Surpassing the Love of Women': Another Look at 2 Samuel 1:26 and the Relationship of David and Jonathan." In *Authorizing Marriage? Canon, Tradition, and Critique in the Blessing of Same-Sex Unions*, edited by Mark D. Jordan, 7–16 Princeton, NJ: Princeton University Press, 2005.

Provan, Iain, et al. *A Biblical History of Israel*. 2nd ed. Louisville, KY: Westminster John Knox, 2015.

Provan, Iain. "Why Barzillai of Gilead (1 Kings 2:7)? Narrative Art and the Hermeneutics of Suspicion in 1 Kings 1–2." *TynBul* 46.1 (1995) 103–16.

Routledge, Robin. "'An Evil Spirit From the Lord'—Demonic Influence or Divine Instrument?" *EvQ* 70 (1998) 3–22.

Schroer, Silvia, and Thomas Staubli. "Saul, David and Jonathan—the Story of a Triangle? A Contribution to the Issue of Homosexuality in the First Testament." In *A Feminist Companion to Samuel and Kings*, edited by Athalya Brenner, 22–36. Sheffield, UK: Sheffield Academic Press, 2000.

Seibert, Eric. *Disturbing Divine Behavior: Troubling Old Testament Images of God*. Minneapolis, MN: Fortress, 2009.

Shemesh, Yael. "David in the Service of King Achish of Gath: Renegade to His People or a Fifth Column in the Philistine Army?" *VT* 57.1 (2007) 73–90.

Ska, Jean Louis. *"Our Fathers Have Told Us": Introduction to the Analysis of Hebrew Narrative*. Rome: Pontifical Biblical Institute, 1990.

Smith, Mark S. *Poetic Heroes: Literary Commemorations of Warriors and Warrior Culture in the Early Biblical World*. Grand Rapids: Eerdmans, 2014.

Bibliography

Smith, Richard G. *The Fate of Justice and Righteousness during David's Reign: Rereading the Court History and Its Ethics according to 2 Samuel 8:15b—20:26*. LHBOTS, Vol. 508. London: T. & T. Clark, 2009.

Spronk, Klass. "Good Death and Bad Death in Ancient Israel According to Biblical Lore." *Social Science and Medicine* 58 (2004): 987–95.

Tsumura, David Toshio. *The First Book of Samuel*. NICOT. Grand Rapids: Eerdmans, 2007.

———. *The Second Book of Samuel*. NICOT. Grand Rapids: Eerdmans, 2019.

VanderKam, James C. "Davidic Complicity in the Deaths of Abner and Eshbaal: A Historical and Redactional Study." *Journal of Biblical Literature* 99.4 (1980) 521–39.

Walsh, Jerome T. *Old Testament Narrative: A Guide to Interpretation*. Louisville, KY: Westminster John Knox, 2009.

Westbrook, April D. *"And He Will Take Your Daughters . . ." Woman Story and the Ethical Evaluation of Monarchy in the David Narrative*. LHBOTS 610. London: Bloomsbury T. & T. Clark, 2015.

Wolpe, David. *David: The Divided Heart*. New Haven, CT: Yale University Press, 2014.

Wray Beal, Lissa M. *1 & 2 Kings*. AOTC 9. Downers Grove, IL: IVP Academic, 2014.

Wright, Christopher J.H. *The God I Don't Understand: Reflections on Tough Questions of Faith*. Grand Rapids: Zondervan, 2008.

Zehnder, Markus. "Observations on the Relationship between David and Jonathan and the Debate on Homosexuality." *WTJ* 69 (2007) 127–74.

AUTHOR INDEX

Abasili, Alexander Izuchukwu, 108n8
Ackerman, Susan, 51
Ackroyd, Peter, 109, 110n11
Alter, Robert, 29, 43, 64n12
Amit, Yairah, 32n16, 123n4, 130n15, 136n23, 154n17
Arnold, Bill T., 114n17
Athas, George, 10n14
Avioz, Michael, 129n13, 137n23
Auerbach, Eric, 3

Baden, Joel S., 1n1
Bar-Efrat, Shimon, 134n21
Barstad, Hans M., 11n17
Becking, Bob, 13n19, 13n21
Bergen, Robert D., 78n6, 88n2, 113n14
Bodner, Keith, 44n5, 58n6, 71n19, 92n7, 99n9, 113n13, 128n11, 130n14, 130n16, 133n19, 136n22, 137n24, 154n16
Borgman, Paul, 4n9, 137, 138, 144n4

Brueggemann, Walter, 80, 81, 81n9, 95n13, 97, 99n18, 148n6, 149n8, 152n12

Chapman, Stephen B., 44n6, 47n8, 56, 57n4, 79, 149n9, 152n13

Daly-Denton, Margaret M., 133n18
Davies, Philip R., 11n16
DeRouchie, Jason S., 10n14
Dever, William G., 13n5, 14, 15

Edelman, Diana Vikander, 77n4
Esler, Philip F., 28n12
Evans, Mary J., 114n17
Evans, Paul S., 47n9, 77, 113n14

Firth, David G., 42n2, 44n5, 46n7, 58n7, 77n5, 78n6, 84n12, 89n3, 95n11, 98n16,

Author Index

Firth, David G. (*continued*)
  106n5, 114n16,
  127n9, 131n17,
  144n4, 145n5,
  148n7
Frontain, Raymond-Jean,
  3n8, 161n1

Galil, Gershon, 13n21
Gilmour, Rachelle, 11n17
Goldingay, John, 71n20
Gordon, Robert P., 68n17,
  98n16, 136n23
Green, Barbara, 59, 144n3,
  169n5
Greenspahn, Frederick E.,
  22n6

Halpern, Baruch, 2n5, 3
Hill, Andrew E., 127n8

Jacobs, Jonathan, 116n23
Johnson, Benjamin J. M.,
  6n11, 9n14, 14n22,
  23n8, 26n10, 29n14,
  33n17, 33n18,
  67n14, 71n19,
  165n2,
Johnson, Vivian L., 72

King, Philip J., 28n11
Knapp, Andrew, 12n18
Koenig, Sara, 108n7

Lamb, David T., 115n21
Lennox, John C., 123n3
Levenson, Jon D., 7, 69,
  115n20
Linafelt, Tod, 89n4
Long, V. Philips, 11n15,
  11n17, 63n10

Mann, Steven Thatcher,
  133n20
Mazar, Amihai, 13n19
Mazar, Eilat, 13n20
McCarter, P. Kyle, Jr.,
  114n18, 125n5,
  128n11, 150n10
Meyers, Carol, 61n9
Millard, Alan, 13n21, 28n11
Miller, Virginia, 129n12
Miscall, Peter D., 83n11
Morrison, Craig E., 100

Noll, K. L., 1

Olyan, Saul M., 51n15

Provan, Iain, 11n15, 11n17,
  157n20

Routledge, Robin, 23n7

Sanders, Paul, 13n21
Schroer, Silvia, and Thomas
  Staubli, 49n12
Seibert, Eric, 115n21
Shemesh, Yael, 82, 83
Ska, Jean Louis, 77n3
Smith, Mark S., 47n11,
  51n14, 52, 53n18
Smith, Richard G., 130n15

Tsumura, David Toshio,
  23n7, 128n11

VanderKam, James C., 93n9

Walsh, Jerome T., 68n16,
  117n24
Westbrook, April D., 92n8,
  95n12

Author Index

Wojcik, Jan, 3n8, 161n1
Wray Beal, Lissa M., 157n19
Wright, Christopher J. H., 115

Zehnder, Markus, 49n13, 51n14

SCRIPTURE INDEX

OLD TESTAMENT

Genesis

8:21	77n3
12:1–4	143
12:11	22n4
15:1–16	143
15:4	98
17:1–21	143
22	115n20
22:16–18	143
24:16	22n5
25:7–11	158
25:25	21
26:7	22n5
27:41	77n3
29:17	22n4
29:31—30:24	20
31:19–35	44
34:19–20	115
39:6	20, 22
39:7–20	20
44:30	41, 50

Exodus

13:13–16	115n20
21:12–14	155n18
25:13–15	94
28:4	61n9
28:15	61n9
28:26	61n9
28:28	61n9
28:30	61n9
34:6–7	115
34:19–20	115n20

Leviticus

8:8	61n9
18:9	124n5
18:11	124n5
18:21	114n19
20:3	114n19
20:17	124n5

Numbers

4:1–18	94
18:15–16	115n20

Deuteronomy

5:8–10	115
7:20	78

Scripture Index

8:17	77n3
10:12–13	41
12:10–11	96
12:10	97
12:30–31	114n19
22:28–29	125n6
23:9–14	109n10
23:10–11	109n10
24:16	115
27:22	124n5

Joshua

13:1–2	78n6
15:44	60

Judges

14:6	22
14:19	22
15:14	22
20:16	33

1 Samuel

1:20	60
2:1–10	145
2:27–36	59
5:3–4	35
6–7	94
6:19	94
7	94n10
8:10	60
8:11	130
8:19–20	28, 106
8:20	35
9	18
9:1	29
9:2	21
10:6	45
10:7	63, 63n10
10:10	22
10:10–12	45
10:23	21
10:24	21
11	18
11:2	22n5
11:6	22
13	18, 19
13:13–14	169
13:14	4, 5, 8, 9, 47, 69, 96, 101, 164, 167
14	57
14:3	59
15	18, 58, 78n6, 82
15:15	19
15:21	19
15:23	18, 44
14:24	114
15:27–29	64n11
15:28	5
15:30	114
16	18, 19
16–17	17, 36
16:1	18
16:1–13	18–23, 37
16:6	5
16:7	6, 8, 17n1, 30, 36, 47, 48, 69, 96, 101, 162, 164, 165
16:12	6, 47, 101
16:13–14	26
16:14–23	23–26, 37
16:18	57n5, 96
16:21	42, 47
16:21–23	36

Scripture Index

1 Samuel (*continued*)

17	26, 40, 91, 162
17:1–11	27–28
17:4–8	20
17:12–31	29–30
17:26	37, 45
17:28	36, 165, 169
17:29	1n4, 46
17:32–40	30–33
17:32	37, 165, 169
17:39	23
17:41–54	33–35
17:45–47	25
17:46–47	77
17:46	37, 65n13
17:47	37
17:48–51	37
17:52	13
17:55–58	35–36
17:55	17n2
18	40–43, 162
18–19	57
18:1	39n1, 47, 50
18:3	46
18:9	47
18:12	23, 96
18:14	23, 96
18:16	47
18:17	56
18:18	99n19
18:20	39n1, 47
18:21–22	56
18:23	99n19
18:28	23, 47, 96
18:29	39n1
18:20	8
19	43–45, 66, 92
19–20	72
19:1	43, 50
20	45–48
20:3	50
20:17	50
20:41	50, 51
21	129, 162
21–22	55–59
21:3 [4MT]	67n15
21:4–5	109n10
22:10	60
22:13	60
22:14	54n1
22:15	60
23	60–62, 77, 84, 162
24	62–66, 148
24	68, 68n17, 69, 71, 162
24:3	72
24:4	73
24:5	72, 151, 166, 169
24:14	25
24:17	54n3, 82
24:19	72, 82
25	6, 7, 8, 66–70, 68n17, 69, 77, 162
25:2–8	6
25:3	22n4
25:10	2, 54n2, 164

Scripture Index

25:21–22	7	6:22	87n1
25:31	101, 151, 166, 169	6:23	8
		7	3, 94, 95–101, 103, 115, 156, 162
25:44	8, 92		
26	62–66, 162, 166		
		7:3	167, 169
26:10	70	7:3–4	154
26:23	82	7:12–16	123
27	76–80	7:18	87n1
27:1	166n3	7:27	133, 167, 169
27:8–12	86		
28	80, 129	8–9	101–2
28:1	79	9–20	167
28:2	80	10:6–18	106
28:16–19	81	10	117–18
29	80–83	11	7, 8, 129, 169
29:5	75n1		
29:8	75n2	11–12	119, 121, 124, 163
30	83–85		
30:1–7	106	11:1–5	105–08
31	88n2	11:1	118
		11:6–13	108–10
2 Samuel		11:14–27a	110–12
1	24, 88–91, 88n2	11:27b—12:12	112–13
		12	118, 119, 129
1:17–27	71, 145		
1:25–26	87n1	12:7	104n1
1:26	48, 51	12:10	119, 122n1, 124, 141
2–5	91–94		
2–3	103		
2:1–4	131	12:10–11	138
2:1–10	89	12:12	134
3:2–5	154	12:13–25	113–17
3:15	8	12:13	104n2, 119, 148
3:16	8		
5:2	106	12:16–18	48
5:3	131	12:24–25	154
5:10	96	12:26–31	117–18
6	8, 94–95	13	124–28, 140
6:21–22	8		

Scripture Index

2 Samuel (*continued*)

13–20	144, 153
13:1	22n4, 124
15:30–31	141
13:33	168, 169
13:39	135, 137
13:39—14:1	135
14	128–29
14:1	136, 168, 169
14:25	22
14:33	136
15:1–12	130–31
15:9	136
15:13—16:14	131–33
15:30–31	135, 148
16:5–13	157
16:15–23	133–34
17:1–22	134–35
18:1—19:15	135–38
18:33	122n2, 137
19:4	48
19:16–43	138–39
19:23	157
20	139–40
21–24	144, 159, 163
21:1–14	145, 150–53
21:15–17	106
21:15–22	145, 149–50
22	24, 145
22:1–51	71, 89, 145–49
23:1–7	71, 89, 145–49
23:5	142n1, 148
23:8–39	145, 149–50
23:39	7
24:1–25	145, 150–52
24	143
24:10	168

1 Kings

1	153–56
1–2	144
1:3	22n4
2	156–59
2:2–3	142n1
2:6	142n2
2:9	142n2
5:3	97
11–12	99
11:29–39	64
12:26	77n3
14:8	1n3, 5, 147
24–25	99

2 Kings

14:6	115

1 Chronicles

22:1	152
22:8	97
28:3	97

Esther

1:11	22n5
2:7	22n4, 22n5
6:6	77n3

Scripture Index

Ecclesiastes

2:15	77n3

Psalms

2:7	99
18	145
51	114
51	119, 121
51:4 [ET]	119
51:9–11 [7–9 ET]	120
51:14 [12 ET]	120
51:8 [6 ET]	120
51:15 [13 ET]	120
51:18 [16–17 ET]	120
52	74
54	74
57	74
106:36–39	114n19
142	71, 73
142:3	72, 73
142:4	72, 73
142:6	72, 73

Song

5:10	20

Jeremiah

19:4–5	114n19
31:30	115

Ezekiel

18:20	115

Hosea

7:2	77n3

Jonah

4:6–11	112

NEW TESTAMENT

Matthew

26:30–46	133n18

Mark

1:11–12	99
14:26–42	133n18

Luke

22:39–46	133n18

Romans

3:28	99n18
6:23	115

1 Corinthians

10:13	83

Galatians

2:16–21	99n18

www.ingramcontent.com/pod-product-compliance
Lightning Source LLC
Chambersburg PA
CBHW031432150426
43191CB00006B/481